ESSENTIALS
FOR
CANCER SURVIVAL

Faith, Family, Friends, Physicians

By
Mike Lynn, PhD

ESSENTIALS FOR CANCER SURVIVAL
Faith, Family, Friends, Physicians
by Mike Lynn, PhD

Printed in the United States of America

ISBN 9781629522968

www.xulonpress.com

Acknowledgements

S pecial hugs for my wife, Kay, for her boundless love, persistence in making me a better person, and being my faith mentor and health advocate.

Thanks to my daughters – the fabulous three – for their unconditional love, patience, understanding, and caring.

Thanks to my brothers, Jay and Jim, and my in-laws, Newt and Judy, for their love, caring, and being available during desperate times of need.

Thanks to my many friends, locally and globally, for their prayers, messages, and visits.

Thanks to Jason for his creative graphic design skills and being a caring nephew.

Thanks to Jane and Celine for their editing wisdom and friendship.

Thanks to the CaringBridge web site for providing a tool for Kay and me to maintain continuous and open communications with our family and friends.

Thanks to the Mayo Clinic professionals for their compassion and medical expertise.

Special eternal thanks to my Lord for providing His grace, mercy, healing, peace, and redemption.

Table of Contents

Preface

This is a true story about how faith, family, friends, and physicians provided hope during my cure from esophageal cancer. This disease is very deadly, with a five-year survival rate of less than 15 percent. While cancer is a devastating physical disease, its impact on one's emotional state can be equally debilitating. In order to deal with the physical issues of cancer, emotional calmness must be realized. This is how spiritual and social support contributes toward a cure.

For my entire pre-cancer life, I had a faith that was more intellect-driven than heart-driven. I believed in salvation through Jesus Christ and that someday I would be with Him in heaven; yet, I did not live my faith. I trusted myself for daily needs rather than trusting in Him. My life was filled with self-confidence, and I believed that I was in control. Then, in the summer of 2007, I was diagnosed with a life-threatening cancer that I could not control. I needed help.

I asked God, "Why me?" I did not know the answer to that question; however, I did know that only God had a plan to use everyone and every experience to further His kingdom. Humbly, I determined that I could not survive without the hope provided only by God. I placed my trust in Jesus Christ, knowing that He would never forsake me, and I asked Christ to be with me and to lead me. I started to live my faith.

I do not have a university degree in theology; therefore, I provide only simple understandings of my spiritual experiences. Where appropriate, I included scripture verses that helped me live through anxious moments, such as this verse from the New Testament.

Be anxious for nothing, but in everything by prayer and supplication with thanksgiving let your requests be made known to God. And the peace of God, which surpasses all comprehension, will guard your hearts and your minds in Christ Jesus.

Philippians 4:6,7 NASB

The encouragement from my family and friends was perhaps the most important worldly influence on my emotional state, as I managed the demanding physical aspects of cancer. Using existing communication technology, it was very easy to connect with support groups. I received thousands of messages, prayers, and visits. I used to believe many of life's challenges could be achieved in isolation. However, now I believe they can be attained only with the inclusion of a compassionate community. When I talked with other cancer patients, they confirmed the importance of a tightly woven network of supporters. My wife, Kay and I were so very grateful to all of our awesome loved ones for their pledge of support to us.

I felt compelled to share my trials, because I knew by talking with other esophageal cancer patients that they, too, had experienced similar challenges. Therefore, I hope this story will help others navigate the many expected and unexpected journeys associated with being a cancer patient. I cannot discount the many unique trials that others encounter. However, this formula for hope can be adapted to overcome most, if not all, of those other distinctive issues. Even possibly, the principles employed for my cure can be tailored to help all patients manage not merely cancer, but all types of life-threatening diseases.

This story was written in chronological order to share the roller coaster ride of the physical, emotional, and spiritual awareness experienced over the course of diagnosis through cure and even into post cure. I chose July 30th, 2007 as day one for my path to cure. That date was not the first time I experienced the symptoms of esophageal cancer. However, that date was the first day I sought medical attention needed to overcome cancer.

Introduction

I was born on April 3rd, 1951 in Greenwich, Connecticut into a loving middle-class, three generations household. We were five children (two girls and three boys), a mom, a dad, and a grandma. The two girls were the bookends in the birth order and I was the fourth child. The children were second generation Americans and baby boomers.

Mom and Dad had a very complementary marriage. Mom stayed home to take care of the household needs and to raise the children. She was a devout Roman Catholic witnessing to God through her obedience to the Catholic doctrine. We attended church every Sunday during the 7:00am Mass. Mom directed the kids to be baptized as infants, blessed in

Holy Communion at age six, and confirmed at age twelve. Mom had extreme patience and a very compassionate heart as she taught us kids how to swim and attended every activity involving her children. Also, Mom taught me how to respect others and how to be a gentleman toward all women. Unfortunately, in 1988, Mom died from kidney failure at the young age of seventy-three. I loved Mom with all my heart.

On the other side of the marriage, Dad was the breadwinner and definitely the head of the family. He had a genius IQ that helped him earn a doctorate in chemical engineering from the Massachusetts Institute of Technology. Logic and correctness were his focus. Dad did not attend church. However, he did have breakfast (scrambled eggs, bacon, and cornbread) prepared every Sunday for our return home from church. He was an avid sports enthusiast with a talent for coaching youth baseball every summer that his boys were eligible to play. Dad was my hero and the Best Man at my wedding. My life would emulate many of his qualities, except his quick-to-flare Irish temper. Dad died from cancer in 1999 at the age of eighty-four.

As in many post-World War II households, my grandma lived with us. My other three grandparents died before Mom and Dad were married. Gram, as we called her, was my mom's mother. My mom would not accept Gram living alone or anywhere else except in our home. This was just one example of my mom's caring heart. For me, having Gram living with us was awesome. As with my mom, Gram was a devout Catholic. She taught us kids faith, tenderness, love, and the importance of extended families. One example of Gram's love was whenever I had a nightmare, I would go directly to Gram's bedroom. She quietly invited me into her bed by raising the blanket and then cuddling me with her soft and protective arm. In 1967, Gram died from colon cancer. That was over four decades ago. To this day, I have not forgotten her voice, her features, the funeral, or the family gathering after the funeral at our house.

By age nine, I was demonstrating above average skills in sports, math, and logic. My siblings, friends, and teachers recognized those skills as they taught me many different types of recreational and educational games. During times off from school, I would enhance my gaming prowess from sunrise to sunset at a local park. I enjoyed every competitive activity. However, the competition was not always about winning. I was more interested in understanding my opponent's thought process and in developing my playing strategy than the immediate satisfaction of winning. My goal was to uncover an advantage enabling victory at future meetings. This approach would guide my behavior for the rest of my life, whether playing games or negotiating business contracts.

By age twelve, my body, especially my knees, started to rebel against all the physical activities. In the summer of 1963, I had the first of six knee operations, culminating at age forty-one with total knee replacements for both the right and left knees.

For me, those knee operations were mere inconveniences because the actual surgical procedures were reasonably painless and the recovery was relatively easy. Those operations, along with a 1976 emergency appendectomy for a burst appendix, helped build my confidence that I could overcome any physical setback.

During my senior year in high school, my parents asked about my intentions for further education. For my family, the question was not whether to attend college or not, but at which college to enroll. At that age, I was too immature to provide a good answer to my parents' question; therefore, my dad took control of the college selection. He phoned a friend who was a college professor at North Carolina State University (NCSU). They talked about my SAT scores, high school grades, and extra-curricular activities. During this phone conversation, I was accepted into the Department of Textile Chemistry with a minor in chemical engineering. After my dad made my college education arrangements for me, I asked him one question, "Where is NCSU?"

My university years were fabulous. I discovered that North Carolina was a beautiful state with coastal beaches, forested mountains, and lots of farmland. The people were gracious and friendly. The university's sports teams were first class, being invited to football post-season bowl games and winning the 1974 NCAA Basketball Championship. Above all, I received a wonderful education. I left NCSU with a BS in Textile Chemistry, a MS in Chemical Engineering, and a PhD in Polymer and Fiber Science. I became a doctor just like my dad.

The NCSU story does not end with my various technical degrees, though. There was one more piece to the story, which happens to be much more important to me than any academic degree. I left NCSU married to a faith-filled Southern belle, Kay. She was also very cute, athletic, and smart. God brought Kay into my life during my senior year, at a time when I felt emotionless, faithless, and uncompromising. Too much of my focus was on studying and science. I needed to find a better balance between school, faith, and social activities. Thankfully, God interceded in my life so that, in 1975, Kay became my wife, spiritual mentor, and lifelong partner.

After graduate school, I needed to find a job. Fortunately, when I received my PhD in 1978, the job market was promising. I received several employment offers from different Fortune 500 companies. I finally accepted an offer from the 3M Company in Minnesota. The company had an excellent reputation and the job assignment was exciting. However, the most important reason for accepting the offer was that my brother, Jay worked for the 3M Company and lived in Minnesota. As Gram taught me, the importance of family was an overriding factor in making any decision. To convince Kay to move to Minnesota, I promised her that within five years we would return to North Carolina, the state we both loved. She believed me and was excited to start a new short-term adventure. Over three decades later, we still live in Minnesota.

In 1979, our first child, Jennifer was born. Kay quit her teaching job to become a full-time stay-at-home mom. Over the next several years, God blessed our marriage with two more awesome daughters, Tracy and Christine. We were becoming similar to my parents with kids of our own and a complementary marriage, except that both Kay and I needed to be integral parts in our children's faith.

At age forty, while on a five-year 3M assignment in Belgium, I was diagnosed with Type 1 Diabetes. The doctors told me that they did not know the reason for me getting diabetes, especially at age forty, but they did know an effective treatment that would allow me to live a normal life. The treatment was for me to prick my finger several times a day to determine the amount of sugar in my blood and then to self-inject a calculated dosage of insulin into my abdomen. I did not know how this would provide a normal life. However, I was confident in being able to control the disease because the treatments were essentially a math game.

Sadness struck my family in 2006. My younger sister, Cathy died of a massive heart attack. She was only forty-five years old. Then, in 2011, my older sister, Maryanne died of cancer. She was sixty-five years of age. At this time, I had lost Gram, Mom, Dad, and both sisters. Psychologically, Gram, Mom, and Dad represented a generational buffer between death and me. That barrier is now gone. My generation is currently the one facing death, as in the cases of my two sisters. The lack of a death shield is very sobering and makes me feel humble and anxious. Indeed, we are all mortal.

In 2007, my cancer story began. My life and the lives of many others would dramatically change.

Chapter 1

Pre-Diagnosis

For me, 2007 started as a very promising year. My family was healthy and my job at 3M Company was stimulating and secure. My middle daughter, Tracy was three months pregnant with my first grandchild. The winter was mild with above average temperatures and below average snowfall, especially for my home state of Minnesota. If golf courses opened early, 2007 was going to be a perfect year.

However, in February, the year started to turn ugly. I was experiencing heartburn symptoms and problems while swallowing. As usual, my scientific nature tried to determine the cause and ultimately, the fix. I thought that maybe I was drinking too much diet soda, which was carbonated and acidic, and possibly causing heartburn and upper abdominal discomfort. When I stopped drinking diet soda, the symptoms disappeared. 2007 was back on track to being a good year.

But, then, the weather turned hostile. Minnesotans had to deal with a double dose of snow in the final week of February and the first day of March. In the two storms, the snow accumulation was more than two feet. I am not a fan of snow because driving becomes treacherous, temperatures are cold, and golf season is delayed. However, by late March, rain washed away the snow and brought moderate temperatures. The winter of 2006-2007 was done. Golf season would start on time, with temperatures reaching the 70s by mid-April.

Then, on June 12th, Micah was born. I was a proud grandpa and 2007 was an awesome year.

In late June, my swallowing issues returned. I mentally noted that dry food, in particular chicken, beef, bread, and rice, was difficult to swallow. I could eat only half of a cheese and mushroom burger before my throat felt clogged. Thankfully, the discomfort disappeared within an hour after eating. I stubbornly decided to ignore the swallowing issues and was sure that it would eventually go away. Besides, I was about to leave on a trip with my youngest daughter, Christine, for a July 4th father-daughter bonding experience.

Christine and I decided to fly to Philadelphia to visit my brother, Jim, and his family. Along with visiting family, we toured historic Philadelphia and drove to the ocean. On this trip, I struggled to eat my brother's delicious meals. In addition, at a famous crab shack on the banks of the Chesapeake Bay, Jim observed that I could not eat much crab, which was quite unusual for me. Beside the swallowing issues, I noticed that I was losing weight. I did not know what to do and was starting to get anxious.

For the first time in my life, I was losing control of my physical and emotional state.

After any new experience, Christine's usual habit was to tell her mom everything. She was a delightful "tell all" fourteen-year-old, and the trip to Philadelphia was no exception. She began by telling her mom how bored she was with seeing the Liberty Bell and finished with her version of my eating problems. As a concerned wife, Kay sat me down to first listen to my side of the story and then to coach me on her thoughts and recommendations.

Her conclusion was that it was time to make an appointment with a doctor. This was not a suggestion or a request, but a loving companion taking control. I had no choice but to comply.

Chapter 2

Diagnosis

D ay 1: Pursuant to Kay's command, I contacted
my general internist. Monday, July 30th, 2007
was his first available appointment. I described to
him my swallowing issues. I was eating only soup,
yogurt, and mashed food. Since I was a diabetic,
keeping my blood sugars in balance with that diet
was taxing. In the forty-five days prior, I lost fifteen
pounds and I was losing weight at an alarming rate
of about half a pound per day. The doctor asked me
about any bleeding issues, but there were no indi-
cations of bleeding. Therefore, his first thought was
that it could be acid reflux, but to be on the cautious

side, he recommended I have an endoscopy to view my esophagus and stomach. That meant that I needed to swallow a camera attached to a tube so that the doctors could see and take pictures of my innards. Even though I was uneasy about the discomfort of an endoscopy, I agreed with the doctor to have this intrusive procedure. By using a thoughtful approach in advising an endoscopy, my general internist probably saved my life.

Day 4: That was the first day available for my endoscopy. The endoscopy surgeon sprayed a topical anesthesia down my throat and then he sedated me. Since I was asked to swallow a camera on the end of a long tube, I thanked God for sedatives. The surgeon advanced the video scope from my mouth into my esophagus and down to my stomach. He saw an ulcerated and friable golf ball-size mass at the junction of my esophagus and stomach (GE junction). The mass was suspicious for malignancy. Therefore, he took five biopsies for pathology testing (laboratory evaluations for cancerous cells).

When I woke from the sedative, the surgeon told me about the findings. After a couple of minutes, the surgeon left the room and then Kay joined me in the recovery room. I sat on the edge of the bed with a broad, happy smile, still partially sedated, as I told Kay they found a tumor in my esophagus. Kay was speechless.

A nurse came into the recovery room to discharge me. The nurse noticed Kay's surprised body language. After a minute or two, Kay asked the nurse if the surgeon was available to meet with us. A few minutes passed before the surgeon re-entered the recovery room. He gave us a four-picture collage of the tumor and told us that the tumor was most likely esophageal cancer, but the pathology results were needed for confirmation. If the biopsies verified cancer, he said that I would have a 5 to 15 percent chance of surviving five years.

Finally, he recommended that I find a premier cancer clinic, because there was not a local medical team experienced enough to help me. Then, the surgeon discharged me. Maybe the frank and concise monologue from the surgeon was not the best bedside manner. However, by telling us straight, the surgeon spoke clearly of the urgency and seriousness of my situation. We had to act on his words without delay. My life and the lives of my family were about to dramatically change.

Kay and I walked out of the hospital in total shock, not knowing what to say or what to do. After a few quiet minutes, I suggested we go to a local coffee shop. Since the month was August, we drank our coffee outside at a table on the patio. I started to cry. Kay held me in her arms and kissed my forehead. Then, she suggested that we needed to pray. That was an awesome suggestion and would affect us for the rest of our lives. We held hands to pray for peace of mind for ourselves and for our family. We prayed for our Lord and Savior to grant us grace and mercy. We prayed for wisdom to make the correct decisions and for strength for me to tolerate the difficult treatments required for curing cancer.

We prayed for God to guide us to the best medical professionals and for God to guide the medical team as they treated my physical needs.

Do not fear, for I am with you;
Do not anxiously look about you,
for I am your God.
I will strengthen you, surely I will help you,
Surely I will uphold you with My righteous
right hand.

Isaiah 41:10 NASB

After we finished praying, we simultaneously felt a warm peace engulf us. Instantly, we knew, whether I survived or died, our Lord would provide for us and for our family. We needed our faith to comfort us and to hold us strong. At that moment, I relinquished absolute control of my life to Jesus Christ.

Peace I leave with you; My peace I give to
you; not as the world gives do I give to you.
Do not let your heart be troubled, nor let it
be fearful.

John 14:27NASB

After coffee, I told Kay that I wanted to tell our family and friends. She asked why they had to know before the cancer was confirmed. I told her that I selfishly needed to talk to my daughters, brothers, and close friends to gain their strength and support. I desired to talk to them face-to-face, especially our daughters, so that they could hear from me about the worrisome diagnosis and they could see that I was still strong enough and willing to fight for my life. They should hear from her and me that the Holy Spirit was within both of us, giving us peace and strength. Soon, my family and friends would find out that I was in trouble, and that Kay and I needed them. I knew that I could not beat this deadly cancer without my faith, family, and friends.

After telling our family and close friends, and after the surprise, tears, and hugs subsided, I was certain they all went to the Internet to research esophageal cancer. Their findings would not be good and would inform them about the deadly disease. In truth, this type of cancer was ugly and the treatments for cure were even uglier. Though they knew I also searched the Internet, my family and friends would not talk about the negatives. They knew I was in a fight for my life. For Kay and me, being transparent and honest at the onset allowed our future conversations with loved ones to be upbeat, which kept me optimistic. They continued to show unconditional love for us.

Day 5: I had an early morning presentation reviewing my work project to executive management at 3M Company. The presentation went fine and the subsequent comments and recommendations from management were positive. Just before management left the meeting room, though, I asked for a few more minutes of their time to disclose a medical issue. I showed them the four-picture collage of the tumor and told them that I was going on medical leave. After I finished, the highest-ranking member of the review team got out of his chair to give me a compassionate hug. He told me that my first and only priority was to get well. In addition, he said that all work-related issues would be taken care of by the rest of the project team.

A few hours after the meeting, I received an unexpected phone call from the 3M Company medical doctor because the senior member of the review team contacted him concerning my medical issue. The doctor offered his help in finding an appropriate medical facility experienced in treating esophageal cancer. For a 21st century Fortune 100 corporation, 3M Company got from me an A+ rating in employee relations and compassion.

Day 6: Kay, Christine, and I drove four hours to Madison, Wisconsin to spend the day with our oldest daughter, Jennifer, and her husband, Jeff. I needed to show them that I was strong enough mentally and physically to beat this cancer. Also, Kay and I wanted to tell them that God was in total control and that He would take care of us now and for eternity. The day was very special. We talked about the cancer, shed some tears, had some laughs, and reassured ourselves of our love and commitment to each other.

The drive home was mentally draining because all I could think about was esophageal cancer and the difficult months ahead for my family and me. I had read too much on the Internet. I was starting to prepare myself for the difficult treatments required for cure. Kay and Christine tried to change my focus with limited success. Finally, after about three hours of driving, we decided to pray. Then, God set my mind at peace.

Day 7: Tracy and her husband, Pastor Chris, set up a prayer service at my home with family and a few very close friends. It was a wonderful time of prayer and praise while turning our fears and anxiety over to God. This was exactly what Kay and I needed.

Day 9: The endoscopy surgeon phoned. He said the pathology results were inconclusive, which meant that even though the biopsy tissue was ulcerated, necrotic, and suspicious of malignancy, cancer cells could not be substantiated. He recommended more biopsies to be taken, which, in laymen's terms, meant that I needed to swallow another camera attached to a tube during an endoscopy procedure.

Day 10: I had a CT scan of my chest, abdomen, and pelvis. Prior to the scan, I drank two pints of barium contrast and was given intravenously 100 cc of an organically bound iodine diagnostic radi-opaque media. The scan was non-intrusive and painless, except for the IV needle prick. I lay flat on a table while the table moved in and out of a relatively small, donut-shaped machine. Drinking the oral contrast was more difficult than the scan. The results of the scan were unremarkable, except for a gall bladder stone. Cancer was not indicated.

Day 12: I had a series of blood tests. Other than my A1C (three month blood sugar indicator) being a bit high, which confirmed my diabetes was being poorly managed by me, there were no evidences of cancer.

Based on the results of the pathology evalua-tions, the CT scan, and the blood tests, my general internist said the tumor must be benign. I asked him about the endoscopy pictures. He had not seen the pictures. Fortunately, I had a copy of the four-picture collage. After looking at the pictures, he said the tumor looked suspiciously like cancer. Even though the testing results did not confirm cancer, the pictures did. My general internist now agreed with the endoscopy surgeon. They needed more biopsies to be taken and then tested. The doctor recommended another endoscopy. This time, the endoscopy would include an ultrasound, which would provide more details of the tumor and surrounding areas, and would include more biopsies for pathology testing. In addition, my general internist gave me a prescription for Prilosec, to try to reduce the occurrence of acid reflux. At that moment, Kay and I knew that our local doctors could not provide the needed expertise to help me, and that we had to find and make an appointment at a premier cancer clinic.

Thankfully, the world renowned Mayo Clinic with a staff of 25,000 was only a one-hour twenty-minute drive from our home. Mayo Clinic was where I had my total knee replacement procedures, meetings with endocrinologists for my diabetes, and routine physical exams. With my twenty-year history at the Mayo Clinic, I had a very high respect for all the medical professionals at the clinic. At that time, I needed to find the correct doctor or doctors at Mayo to care for my cancer. One of Kay's and my very best friends, Dan, had many business contacts at the Mayo Clinic. When Dan heard of my situation, he offered to help me find an appropriate Mayo doctor. Within a couple of days, I had a name and an address at the Mayo Clinic to contact. Without hesitation, I boldly sent a letter, including test results and scans, to the doctor, describing my medical situation and asking for an appointment as soon as his calendar permitted. I also included with the letter my Mayo Clinic ID number. I prayed for acceptance to the Mayo Clinic.

Save me, O God,
For the waters have threatened my life.
I have sunk in deep mire,

and there is no foothold;
I have come into deep waters,
and a flood overflows me...
May the flood of water not overflow me
Nor the deep swallow me up,
Nor the pit shut its mouth on me.
Answer me, O Lord,
for Your lovingkindness is good;
According to the greatness of Your
compassion, turn to me,
And do not hide Your face from Your servant,
For I am in distress; answer me quickly.

Psalm 69:1-2, 15-17 NASB

Also, that day, Jennifer set up an account for me on the CaringBridge web site. The CaringBridge site is for sick people where up-to-the-minute journals, guest book entries, and tributes are documented. Kay and I used this site to maintain continuous, transparent, and easy access communications with our family and friends. We wrote a journal entry every few days to document my trials and current situation. This allowed family and friends to be updated on my condition before any visit or phone call. Then, when they talked to Kay or me, they used the precious time to encourage, strengthen, and love us without the need to discuss the negative aspects of cancer. Throughout my cancer story, the CaringBridge site would prove to be a valuable communication tool. Between diagnosis and cure, my CaringBridge site was accessed by loved ones more than 7,000 times.

Day 15: As we waited for the Mayo Clinic doctor to reply, I underwent another endoscopy that was ordered by my internist, but this time including an ultrasound. The results indicated a worrisome mass at the GE junction with two enlarged lymph nodes adjacent to the esophagus and the stomach and, of course, a gall bladder stone. The findings were very suspicious for esophageal cancer with regional lymph node metastases (transmission of esophageal cancer cells from the esophagus to lymph nodes). A few more biopsies were taken for pathology testing.

Day 24: A thoracic surgeon with esophageal cancer experience at the Mayo Clinic graciously accepted me as his patient, with my first appointment including blood tests and an endoscopy, along with ultrasound and biopsies. Even though the doctor had the reports from my previous endoscopies and CT scan, he insisted on another endoscopy done the "Mayo way." For the third time in less than a month, I was asked to swallow a camera attached to a long tube. This was not fun, but I understood the need for repetitive testing. The results of this endoscopy confirmed the results of the other two. I had a tumor in my esophagus with two enlarged lymph nodes adjacent to the esophagus and, of course, a gall bladder stone. In other words, I had cancer.

Day 25: The next step was to have a PET scan to determine if the cancer had metastasized anywhere else in my body. For a PET scan, the technician injected radioactive sugars into my arm. Then I was told to completely rest for forty-five minutes with my eyes closed while sitting on a recliner in an isolated area, with soft music playing. The intent was to not use any muscles. Since cancer cells require more food than normal cells, the radioactive sugars would be consumed by the cancer cells and then, during the scan, the cells that consumed the radio-active sugars would light up the PET scan screen. If muscles were in use, the healthy muscle cells would consume the radioactive sugars, causing false positives. After the forty-five-minute wait, the PET scan was done, similar to a CT scan, by having me recline flat on a table while the table moved in and out of a small, donut-shaped machine. The results of this PET scan confirmed cancer in the lower portion of the esophagus, the upper portion of the stomach, and two adjacent lymph nodes. There was no evidence of cancer anywhere else in my body. Thankfully, the cancer was localized.

By knowing the results of the endoscopy and scans, the Mayo doctors explained to Kay and me the treatment plan for my cancer. The treatment was twenty-eight days of radiation with chemotherapy at the beginning and end of radiation, followed by a surgical procedure six weeks later. The doctors reiterated that this cancer was extremely aggressive and deadly.

As we drove home, Kay asked how I felt. She was not asking about my physical condition, but was asking about my emotional state. I told her that I still was at peace, knowing Christ was with us. I added that I was a bit anxious to get the treatments started. However, I was not looking forward to the discomfort and side effects of radiation and chemo. Furthermore, I said that I was okay with the treatment plan, knowing that she was at my side, acting as my advocate, and providing me with love. Finally, we promised each other to pray together every time we drove to the Mayo Clinic. Then, I fell asleep.

The Lord is my rock and my fortress
and my deliverer,
My God, my rock, in whom I take refuge;
My shield and the horn of my salvation,
my stronghold.
       Psalm 18:2 NASB

Day 26: I was sent to a radiation oncologist to get prepared for radiation. The doctor showed Kay and me the radiation equipment and introduced us to the technicians assigned to the equipment. The technicians made me lie on a table with my arms resting above my head. They put my arms and head in a form-fitting mold. They would use this personalized mold every time I had a radiation treatment so that my head and arms would not move. Also, I was tattooed with inked pinpricks in the center, the right side, and the left side of my abdomen. For each of the twenty-eight radiation procedures, the radiation equipment adjusted to my body and the three tattoos. This focused the radiation precisely on the cancer. The location and size of my cancer was very close to several major organs, including the heart, lungs, liver, and spine. Therefore, the radiation treatment did not have any degrees of freedom for mistakes. The accuracy required for the radiation treatments was another example of the need to utilize a premier cancer clinic.

Just after I was tattooed, the radiation oncologist called for an immediate meeting. It seemed that the pathologist identified the biopsy tissues as non-Hodgkin's lymphoma instead of esophageal cancer. This was fantastic news because non-Hodgkin's lymphoma is not life-threatening. It would still be a serious disease, considering the size of the tumor, but I would live. The treatment plan was about to change and the probability for survival was about to increase significantly. Finally, we had some good news!

After our meeting with the radiation oncologist, Kay and I met a hematologist, a doctor who works with lymphoma patients. He told us that there are over 100 subtypes of lymphoma. At this time, the doctors did not know which type of lymphoma I had. Therefore, they needed to do more tests, including more biopsies, which meant I would have to swallow that camera for a fourth time. Before we left his office, he scheduled me to get more blood tests, an echocardiogram (heart evaluation), an electrocardiogram (heart evaluation), and a bilateral bone marrow biopsy (determine if cancer was in my bone marrow). In addition, he scheduled me to meet with an endocrinologist to evaluate the status of my diabetes and my kidneys. All the scheduled tests and meetings would be for the next week because this meeting took place late Friday afternoon. We left the doctor's office for the one-hour twenty-minute drive home. We had a weekend to spend time with family and friends, rest, and digest the week's findings.

Day 29: The two cardiograms were easy. They indicated my heart was healthy. However, the bone marrow biopsy was not pleasant, requiring a general anesthetic because of the pain induced from taking two different bone marrow samples out of my pelvic bone using a huge needle. After I woke from the sedative, the doctors gave me some pain medicine, which I appreciated. The bone marrow was unremarkable. I had a good heart and no evidence of cancer in my bone marrow. This was more good news!

Day 31: I had more blood tests, and then we met with an endocrinologist. The doctor concluded that my diabetes was under as good control as could be expected, considering my cancer situation. Also, my kidneys were healthy. This doctor cautioned us about the side effects of chemotherapy on diabetics, especially if steroids were used. He said my blood sugars would increase significantly. When that happened, I was to increase my insulin dosage two or three times the normal, as needed. This increase in blood sugar would affect my short-term diabetes control, but, thank God, it would not negatively impact my long-term diabetic health. As I underwent treatments, the doctor promised to help me control my diabetes.

Day 33: I was scheduled for another early morning endoscopy. However, the results of my blood tests came back and it turned out that my potassium level was too high to perform the endoscopy. The doctors told me that potassium was a chemical element that was critical to the function of nerve and muscle cells, including the heart. Having a high potassium level in the blood could be dangerous, especially during a surgical procedure like an endoscopy. I was given some medicine to reduce the potassium level. After a few hours, another blood sample was taken with similar results as the first test. The endoscopy was canceled. The doctors gave me more medicine to take over the weekend, to try to reduce the potassium level. Since this weekend was Labor Day weekend, the doctors rescheduled the endoscopy for Wednesday, September 5th.

Thank goodness for an extended Labor Day weekend. This gave Kay and me needed time at home away from doctors and medical tests. We had time to relax, re-energize ourselves, and spend time with family and friends. Tracy and Micah visited, giving me the chance to hold my grandson as he slept. Several friends came over to walk with me in the neighborhood, to watch the Sunday football games, to play a game of chess, and to simply sit next to me for a casual chat. During this time of crisis, family and friends were irreplaceable. They helped to clear Kay's and my thoughts from cancer and replace those thoughts with laughter and conversations about their lives and other random topics. This time was very important and helpful to us.

What a journey this had been, with many twists and turns! God was so faithful by giving us hope and encouragement when we needed it. We would have been basket cases without the peace that only could come from Him. We had our moments, but in general, we felt calm and had accepted what had come our way, even sometimes with laughter.

I waited patiently for the Lord;
And He inclined to me and heard my cry.
He brought me up out of the pit of destruc-
tion, out of the miry clay, And He set my feet
upon a rock making my footsteps firm.
Psalm 40:1-2 NASB

Day 37: We were back at the Mayo Clinic for more blood tests. The results showed normal potassium levels. I was cleared for an endoscopy on September 5th. Again, I had to be sedated and swallow a camera. The intent of this endoscopy was to take more biopsies to determine the lymphoma subtype.

Day 38: During the endoscopy, the tumor, which now occupied more than half the circumference of my esophagus and was extremely friable and oozing, started to bleed. After about fifteen minutes, the bleeding stopped. The doctor decided to exit the area without taking any biopsies, for fear the bleeding would restart. The doctor concluded the tumor was growing and becoming more aggressive. We hoped that the myriad of testing would stop soon, enabling the treatments to start.

Day 39: Kay and I had a meeting with my primary Mayo doctor, the thoracic surgeon. That was the doctor to whom I sent the letter requesting help at the Mayo Clinic. He was the lead doctor for my Mayo medical team. Kay and I sat in his office, thinking the cancer was non-Hodgkin's lymphoma. We felt good about the prognosis. However, the doctor pulled his chair next to me and he became very serious. He said, "You have esophageal cancer, a very serious disease. You have the fight of your life ahead of you." Kay and I no longer felt good but felt overcome with fear. We held hands.

Even though the pathology results did not confirm the exact type of cancer, the Mayo doctors believed it was esophageal cancer because of the tumor's location, size, aggressive behavior, and appearance. Also, the doctors had years of experience diagnosing different types and sub-types of cancer. They had to use their clinical as well as relational expertise to identify the cancer. The doctors called the cancer poorly differentiated because the particular kind of cancer could not be established. I had to trust the Mayo doctors, but more importantly, I had to trust that the Lord had provided the doctors with the correct course of action.

Thirty-eight days had passed since the first doctor's appointment with my general internist. During that time, my family and I had endured a roller coaster of significant stress and relief. First, I was diagnosed with acid reflux and next with a malignant tumor. After that, I was diagnosed with a benign tumor and then again with a malignant tumor. Later, I was diagnosed with non-Hodgkin's lymphoma. Finally, we had a clear diagnosis. The tumor was three-fourths in my esophagus and one-fourth in my stomach, and the cancer had metastasized into two adjacent lymph nodes. The tumor was sized as T3N1M0, which meant the tumor spread to the outer layer of the esophagus, the cancer metastasized to adjacent lymph nodes, and the cancer had not yet metastasized to other major organs. The cancer was stage 3B locally advanced poorly differentiated adenocarcinoma esophageal cancer. I had less than a 15 percent chance of survival. The treatments would start five days later on Tuesday, September 11th, 2007.

Kay and I were mentally and physically exhausted. We needed our faith for strength and to lay our anxiety into the merciful hands of our Lord and Savior. We wanted our family and friends gathered around us to provide love, support, and encouragement. We required our medical team to provide the necessary medical treatments for the cancer and for any unpredictable side effects of the treatments.

Most importantly, we needed each other and the next five days prior to the start of chemotherapy and radiation to relax, re-energize, and regain our mental fitness.

Chapter 3

Preparing For The Worst

While waiting for the cancer treatments to start, I needed something to do to relieve my current anxiety. That something could be simply busy work or it could have value to me and my family. My mind started to consider different options. One very essential duty, I had decided, was finding a way to protect my family and myself in case I died. That task was important, could be accomplished within a few days, and would focus my mind on something other than cancer. That was good.

According to esophageal cancer statistics, I had an 85 percent likelihood of dying within the next five years. That was scary. Before treatments started, I decided to design and implement a low-risk plan to safeguard my family's financial security. Also, I had to continue to pursue a path for eternal life with my Lord. Unfortunately, I had only a few days to complete this mission. Treatments would start in five days, which would undoubtedly affect my ability to think efficiently.

In my young fifty-six years of life, none of my experiences had prepared me for this moment – or had they? Which of my experiences could I draw upon for help? Well, my grandma, mom, dad, and younger sister had passed. I could use the understanding gained from the length of their illnesses and from any of the money or legal issues we had to manage regarding their estates. I could use the logical thinking and problem-solving skills taught to me during my years in school. In addition, I could seek advice from my closest friends. Those experiences helped me plan for the financial and legal issues as follows:

- I reread my "Last Will and Testament." Kay was my personal representative of the entire residue of my estate. That was okay.

- I did not have a health care directive; therefore, I had to execute an "Advanced Directive and Durable Power of Attorney for Health Care," designating Kay as my agent.

- Kay and I reviewed my life insurance policy. The money was sufficient to pay off all our debt, to pay for Christine's college education, and to leave money for the family's future needs. That was okay.

- My retirement account (401-K) was at a maximum contribution, but it was invested in high-risk funds. Based on advice from my brother, Jay, and a couple of friends, I reallocated all the money into a lower risk "Stable Value Fund." In hindsight, that was a good decision because it protected our assets from the eventual 2008/2009 recession.

- Kay and I re-evaluated our available cash and our bond and equity holdings. The cash and bond funds were okay. However, for our current situation, the equity investments were too risky. Therefore, I reallocated all the stock assets to lower risk mutual balanced funds.

- I entered all the asset distributions into an easy-to-read spreadsheet, including fund management contact information. I explained the spreadsheet to Kay. She was comfortable with the overall plan and the spreadsheet.

- Finally, if Kay and my family needed extra money, I knew Kay could get a job. She was smart, articulate, and well educated, plus she could resume her teaching career or find another job of her liking. Kay was resourceful. Also, her skills, personality, and attitude were marketable. I was confident that Kay would be okay.

Now, if I died, would I have eternal life with my Lord? Kay, my spiritual mentor, and I discussed our faith. Both of us considered ourselves to be committed disciples of Christ. We promised one another to continue our growth in Christ, because we knew by believing and following God's Word and serving Him wholeheartedly, that eternal life was promised by God.

> *And the testimony is this, that God has given*
> *us eternal life, and this life is in His Son.*
> *He who has the Son has the life;*
> *he who does not have the Son of God does*
> *not have the life.*
> *These things I have written to you who*
> *believe in the name of the Son of God, so*
> *that you may know that you have eternal life.*
> *1 John 5:11-13 NASB*

At that moment, I was comfortable with my family's financial security and God's promise of eternal life for me. I was ready for the start of treatments.

Chapter 4

Treatments

Kay and I were amazed by the responses from friends as they found out about the schedule for my cancer treatments. We received hundreds of e-mails, letters, cards, and CaringBridge notes. Our neighbors set up a weekly schedule to mow our lawn and tend our garden. Our refrigerator and freezer were filled with many ready-to-eat meals prepared by close friends. We were indeed blessed by the outpouring of love.

I had a choice as to where to receive my treatments. Kay and I decided to use the Mayo Clinic. We could have used a local clinic with the guidance from Mayo doctors. However, considering the precision necessary for the radiation and the effect of chemo on my diabetes, we wanted to use the best-of-the-best at the Mayo Clinic. That decision meant we either commuted to the clinic every day, or stayed near the clinic in a motel or the Hope Lodge, which is American Cancer Society-sponsored free lodging for patients receiving chemo and radiation.

We decided to commute by car the two hours and forty minutes of round trip every day because I wanted as much contact with my kids and grandchild as possible, and I did not want to be surrounded by cancer patients and other sick people 24/7. Since I was physically unable to drive a car, Kay needed help with driving, because she could not be away from home every day. Thankfully, my two brothers offered to stay at our home for two weeks each to help with driving to the Mayo Clinic. At the time of their offer, my brothers did not realize that they were also agreeing to work on Kay's "honey do" list.

With my brothers driving, that allowed Kay to stay home with Christine, who was only fourteen; however, for days when doctors' meetings were scheduled, Kay would join me for the discussions. As for me, I needed to be driven to Mayo every day. The drive provided time for me to bond with the driver, watch the progress of the corn and soybean harvest, or simply take a nap. It also helped that the drive was very scenic.

My older sister, Maryanne wanted to come to Minnesota to help us. However, she had debilitating arthritis, which restricted her ability to travel. Throughout my illness, she maintained contact via the phone.

Day 44: Kay and I met with the radiation oncologist. We asked him point blank if we were going for the cure. With some excitement in his voice, he said, "Absolutely!"

That was the first day of my treatments for cure, which started with radiation. For the radiation treatment, I reclined flat on my back on a table with my head and arms resting in the form fitted mold so as not to move during the treatment. The technicians then adjusted my body in order to align the three tattoos with the equipment. Then, the radiation machine rotated around my midsection, making stops at my back, both sides, and front to apply the radiation beam. The entire process took about ten minutes. The first of the deadly cancer cells were being killed. Bravo for radiation! For that first week, the doctors scheduled radiation for five consecutive days, which included Saturday. The standard for the Mayo Clinic was not to schedule treatments for a Saturday. However, they wanted to hit the tumor aggressively, especially the first week.

That day, the nurses also put a PICC line into my right upper arm. A PICC line is essentially a catheter put into a vein and then precisely threaded in the vein until the tip is close to the heart. This allowed the chemo, after it was connected to the PICC line, to infuse quickly throughout my body. After the PICC line was inserted, the technicians took a chest X-ray to make sure the PICC line was in the proper position. Once the X-ray confirmed the line was positioned correctly, the nurses cautioned me to maintain a keen watch for any arm or hand swelling. Since the PICC line was a foreign body and was in my vein for several days, blood clots could form, causing my arm to swell. If swelling occurred, I was instructed to seek immediate medical care.

Day 45: That was a long day. In the morning, I had my second radiation treatment; that was easy. In the afternoon, chemo started. The nurses asked me if I wanted to recline in a bed or sit in a soft, comfortable chair. Thankfully, I chose a bed, because during the chemo infusion, I got very sleepy and my whole body became very cold, requiring three warm blankets to keep me from freezing. The first step for the infusion was to give me some nausea medicine. Then, they gave me the first chemo, which contained a medicine called cis-platinum. The infusion through the PICC line took four hours.

After complete infusion of the first chemo, the nurse connected the PICC line to a portable pump with a full reservoir of the second chemo, which contained another medicine called 5-FU. I had to carry the pump in a fanny pack for four days as it pumped the second chemo into my body. The pump and I became buddies. For the four days, I did not sleep well for fear of disconnecting from the pump, which fortunately never happened.

Thank the Lord for the five relaxing days prior to the treatments, because I did not react well to chemo. I needed all my strength and courage to endure chemo and the subsequent side effects. My diabetes got out of control and my blood glucose levels hit a staggering high of 600 mg/dl (normal range is 90 to 110). Nausea hit me with vengeance. I could eat and drink very little, thus starting my difficulties with dehydration.

Day 47: Kay and I explained my chemo side effects problems to the Mayo doctors. They changed my nausea medicine, told me to drink as much fluid as possible, and suggested I increase my insulin dosage to as much as two-and-a-half times the normal. Immediately, I made the changes as advised by the doctors, and within a day, I started to feel better. After this tough episode, I knew that the treatments would be difficult. I needed my medical team and my faith to survive these treatments.

*No temptation (trial) has overtaken you
but such as is common to man; and God
is faithful, who will not allow you to be
tempted beyond what you are able, but
with the temptation will provide the way
of escape also, so that you will be able to
endure it.*

1 Corinthians 10:13 NASB

Day 49: Pursuant to the Mayo nurses' instructions, Kay and I disengaged the chemo pump. I was done with the first cycle of chemo. We had a reprieve from driving to the Mayo Clinic because it was Sunday and no radiation treatment was scheduled. My brother, Jay arrived from Phoenix. Other than getting the hiccups and a mild case of thrush (mouth fungus caused by chemo), I was feeling good.

Day 50: Jay drove me to the Mayo Clinic for radiation and removal of the PICC line. I had no hand or arm swelling, which meant no blood clot. However, the unusual happened. After returning from the Mayo Clinic, I took a one-hour nap. Since I did not sleep well the night before, the nap was necessary to re-energize myself. When I woke up, I needed to go to the bathroom. On my way to the bathroom, I became dizzy and blacked out. A few minutes later, I found myself on the floor of the bathroom with a big knot on the side of my head. I crawled on my belly back to bed and then yelled for help with no reply. Jay was two stories below me, napping, Kay was at the store, and Christine was at school. I started to pray.

Then, I heard the garage door open. Tracy had come for a visit. I shouted for her help, so she ran up the stairs to my bedroom, where I asked her to get Jay. Finally, Tracy and Jay started to evaluate me.

They asked several questions and admired the big knot on the side of my head. Everything seemed okay. They determined that I must have hit my head on the bathtub as I was falling. When Kay got home, she froze my head with an icepack to reduce the painful swelling. Kay phoned the Mayo Clinic to inform them of what had happened and to ask for advice. The doctors told Kay that everything sounded okay. However, since I might have a concussion, she should wake me every two hours during the night to check on me. Since I was having trouble sleeping at night, I told Kay that I would wake her every two hours, which I did.

Day 51: After a night of sleep deprivation and waking Kay every two hours, I got up in the morning with a headache and a big knot on the side of my head. Kay froze my head with another icepack. Jay and I drove to the Mayo Clinic for my Tuesday radiation treatment. I showed the doctor my head. He checked me out and commented that my head felt very cold. I told him that Kay froze my head with icepacks. He laughed. I was okay. Thankfully, I did not have a concussion.

That night, Kay sat me down for a long discussion, although lecture was probably a better word. She knew that most of the time I tried to self-resolve my ailments, which was consistent with the male gender. Also, I tended to tell the doctors what I thought they should know, versus telling them everything. I thought too many details would confuse them. Well, the fall in the bathroom and suggestions from Kay changed my attitude. I needed to come clean to both Kay and the doctors. Kay told me that secrets, self-control, and pride were not part of the cure for cancer.

Day 52: Kay drove me to the Mayo Clinic for my radiation, but more importantly, to meet with the doctor. I told the doctor that I felt dizzy, did not have much energy, did not have an appetite, and was losing weight. He quickly realized that I was very dehydrated and considered that my blood chemistry was out of balance. The nurses took some blood and then they gave me one-and-a-half liters of saline solution intravenously. The nurses tried four times to find an open vein for the IV needle before they were successful, which was a strong indication of extreme dehydration. Additionally, the doctor prescribed a different nausea medicine. On a positive note, the results of the blood tests were normal. After the saline solution infusion, I felt great. That night, I slept well for the first time in a while.

Day 53: That day was probably the best day for me in the past several weeks. In the morning, I woke up without nausea or hiccups. I ate a healthy breakfast comprised of a scrambled egg, a cheese sandwich, and milk blended with Carnation Instant Breakfast, which provided extra calories and protein. For lunch at the Mayo Clinic cafeteria, I ate vegetable soup and a bacon-lettuce-tomato sandwich. Well, maybe I did not have a BLT because I gave Jay the bacon and left the lettuce on the plate. I guess I had a tomato sandwich. The ability to actually eat breakfast and lunch was significant. For the previous month, I was not able to eat much, especially not sandwiches. In fact, I lost eleven pounds just in the past week. Maybe eating the sandwiches started a good trend.

I felt so good that day that Jay and I had an entertaining conversation to and from the Mayo Clinic. After returning from the clinic, I took a two-hour nap. For dinner, I had a chicken pot pie with Carnation Instant Breakfast. I thought that the tumor was shrinking, allowing me to eat solid foods. Regardless, it was an exceptionally good day.

Day 55: I struggled with 24/7 hiccups, heartburn, and overall discomfort. Medication, food, and drink did not help. A backrub from Kay, even though very pleasant, did not help. I could not find inner strength to help. Therefore, I turned to my Lord with prayer.

True believers will understand what I am about to write. Non-believers should seriously consider what I am about to write. I prayed to my Lord for His healing touch to do away with the heartburn. Within a minute, I vomited everything that was in my stomach. The heartburn completely stopped. I believe my Lord took the source of heartburn out of my body.

Then, I continued to pray for the hiccups to stop. Simultaneously, Jay and I had a similar thought: maybe ice cream and peanut butter would stop the hiccups. We heard from one of the Mayo doctors a few days ago that he ate peanut butter crackers to relieve his hiccups. Well, crackers were too dry for me to eat; however, ice cream with peanut butter was fluid enough for me to eat. Therefore, Jay fixed me some chocolate ice cream with peanut butter, and after I ate three bites, the hiccups stopped. Was stopping the heartburn and the hiccups a coincidence? I believe not. God provided grace and mercy.

The Lord's lovingkindnesses indeed
never cease,
For His compassions never fail.
      Lamentations 3:22 NASB

For anyone interested in a cure for the hiccups, I suggest a half cup of chocolate ice cream with one teaspoon of peanut butter. Now, I am not talking about just ordinary ice cream right out of the freezer. One must microwave the ice cream for ten seconds to remove the chill, and the peanut butter for seven seconds to be poured over the ice cream. Not only does the remedy work, but it tastes good, too. With this cure, I think I am a potential candidate for the Nobel Prize in Medicine!

Day 59: Kay and I drove to the Mayo Clinic for what we thought was a short meeting with the doctor and a ten-minute radiation treatment. The first sign of the unexpected was at 10:30am when Christine phoned from school that she was ill. Thankfully, Jay was at home to pick up Christine.

The next sign of the unexpected was when the radiation treatment took about thirty minutes instead of ten minutes, because the technicians needed to recalibrate the equipment to my tattoos using a series of X-rays. Luckily, my bones had not moved; thereby, the calibration was a success.

The third and final unexpected event was when the doctor ordered a four-hour IV fluids infusion because I was dehydrated. The infusion was to start at 5pm, which meant that we would leave the clinic no earlier than 9pm. Kay, as a devoted mom, needed to be home to care for her daughter. We had a dilemma. Kay came up with an easy solution when she asked Jay to drive to the clinic starting at 3pm and, at the same time, she left the clinic to drive home. At about 3:40pm, they flashed past each other on Highway 52. Jay tried to spot Kay driving on the highway, but it was impossible to catch a glimpse of the lead-footed Kay on a mission.

With Kay and Jay traveling, I was left alone at the clinic for almost an hour-and-a-half. What if something happened to me? Would the Mayo medical team be able to handle an emergency without my support team? Thankfully, the Mayo team was not challenged because the alone time was uneventful. I even managed to get the infusion started at 3:30pm instead of 5pm, because of a cancellation. That time, the nurses dripped two liters (half gallon) of fluid into me. That was a lot of fluid. Needless to say, my night sleep was interrupted a few times due to the call of nature.

Day 60: I had my 14th radiation treatment. Fourteen are half of twenty-eight. I was halfway finished with radiation. Hooray!

Day 62: Kay asked a very thoughtful question. When talking to loved ones and writing the journal entries in the CaringBridge site, why didn't I mention the pain, fatigue, and emotional lows that I had experienced since the diagnosis? I told her that I needed to share those thoughts and experiences with only her because she needed to help me adjust medications, monitor my intake of fluids and nutrients, and to clearly explain my condition to the doctors. I apologized to Kay for burdening her with all my ups and downs, including the few times I cried in her arms. However, I needed her strength, intuition, and love to get me through these trying times. We were living this life-threatening challenge together.

For a complete answer to Kay's question, I explained that I did not share everything with others, especially my emotional lows, because I needed to focus on the positive. By talking or writing about the negatives, I spent too much time thinking negatively. I had to maintain my inner strength, which came from optimism, humor, and hope. For me to win the battle against cancer, I had to focus on three essential fundamentals. They were my faith, my support team, and my desire to win. After our discussion, I believed Kay finally understood my thinking and welcomed my openness with her.

Also, that day, Jay left for his home in Phoenix. He had been with us for thirteen days. He supported us with grace, compassion, love, and helping hands. He was truly a wonderful brother.

Day 65: Jim, my brother from Philadelphia, arrived. We surprised him at the airport. Instead of one person and one car, we greeted him with three people and two cars. The reason was that I needed to be driven to Mayo immediately after his arrival. Jim felt good enough after the flight to drive me to Mayo. Therefore, after greetings and hugs, Kay and Tracy took one car home, and Jim and I departed with the other car to Mayo for my radiation treatment.

Day 66: Dehydration continued to be my Achilles' heel. When dehydrated, I felt yucky, which was not a medical term, but it best described my condition. After receiving intravenous fluids, I felt young and ready for the next obstacle. Kay knew this well. Therefore, she was a strong spokesperson for regularly scheduled hydration treatments. During our scheduled meeting with the doctor, he quickly realized that he was out-maneuvered and outgunned by Kay. Kay got what she wanted. IV fluids were then scheduled for every fourth day until radiation was complete. Kay was my health zealot and advocate.

Day 67: Jim drove me to the Mayo Clinic for radiation. Before the radiation treatment, the doctor called us into his office for a discussion and told us of yet another development. That development was expected by the doctor but not by me. The results of my weekly blood tests, which were taken the day before, were good. They included a healthy level of white blood cells. However, my neutrophil count was dangerously low, being 650 instead of the normal greater than 2500. A neutrophil is a part of the white blood cell that fights disease, so a low neutrophil count meant that I would not be able to fight infections and diseases. A neutrophil count of less than 500 is extremely dangerous. The doctor told us that my radiation treatments for that day and the next were cancelled and I needed to isolate myself from any sick people until my neutrophil level increased.

The nurse made me put on a facemask. Needless to say, I became very frustrated. The doctor requested daily blood tests to monitor the neutrophil count. I convinced him to start the testing that day. Therefore, I had my blood tested priority 1 status, which meant my blood sample was tested ahead of all other samples in the queue. Jim tried to boost my spirits and helped me refocus on the positive. Also, he told me to phone Kay to let her know of that development. As soon as I told Kay, she started to pray. Before we left the Mayo Clinic, the doctor phoned me for another meeting. He let us know the neutrophil count was 1200 and the next day's radiation treatment was reinstated. I was back on plan. Praise the Lord! The power of prayer and the grace of God provided another miracle.

> *Therefore let us draw near with confidence*
> *to the throne of grace, so that we may*
> *receive mercy and find grace to help in*
> *time of need.*
> *Hebrews 4:16 NASB*

Before we left the doctor's office, he told us that even though I was cleared for radiation, the neutrophil count had to continue to increase. The doctors would not start my next cycle of chemo unless my neutrophil count was above 1500. Chemo was scheduled to start in six days.

Day 71: Kay and I drove to the Mayo Clinic for radiation, blood tests, and an IV fluid fill-up. At this point in the treatment schedule, the radiation and chemo seemed to be working. I was able to eat and drink without discomfort, and I even ate pizza for lunch, which was the first time in three months. The tumor must be shrinking allowing food to pass. Also, the blood test results were excellent with my neutrophil count at 2730. That meant that I took off my facemask and chemo was back on schedule starting in two days.

Day 73: Kay and I drove to Mayo for radiation, the insertion of another PICC line, and the start of my second chemo cycle. The radiation treatment was fine, but the insertion of the PICC line was not pleasant. The nurse inserted the PICC line into my right arm. However, it would not thread in the vein past my shoulder. Something was preventing it from completely threading in the vein to the proper location just near the heart. The nurse did not know what was wrong. He tried two more times before yielding to his supervisor. The supervisor tried once in the right arm, with similar results, and then he tried my left arm with success. The chest X-ray showed the PICC line was in the proper position. I was ready for chemo. To this day, we still do not know the cause of the stoppage in the right shoulder.

That second chemo cycle was similar to the first cycle, with a four-hour infusion of cis-platinum and with me leaving Mayo attached by the PICC line to a portable pump containing 5-FU. Upon our arrival home, we were surprised to see our daughter, Jennifer.

Knowing that I had problems during the first chemo cycle, she came to help. Jennifer had always been a comfort and blessing to Kay and me. As a matter of fact, all three of our daughters were awesome. Due to Tracy living within six miles of us, she continued to do special errands for Kay and visited me several times a week. Christine, who still lived with us, took many walks with me and made sure my water glass was always full. Our three precious daughters lived my cancer with Kay and me. We called them the fabulous three.

The next four days of chemo were almost unbearable. From all the radiation and chemo, I started to get mouth sores and my esophagus felt burned, like a sunburn, but inside my throat. For pain relief, the nurses gave me a special drink that numbed my mouth and esophagus. On the second day, I fainted, but that time, I did not get hurt. Then, my diabetes got out of balance, I had severe nausea, and I had hiccups 24/7, but that time a friend who was an oncology nurse recommended a drug named Baclofen to help stop the hiccups. Baclofen worked! Somehow, and with the care from my family and my Lord, I got through the second and final chemo cycle.

Day 77: Kay disconnected me from the chemo pump. Also, Jim went back home. I was so very blessed to have such an awesome brother.

Day 80: Kay and I drove to Mayo for the 28th and final radiation treatment, more blood tests, a doctor's meeting, an IV fluids fill-up, and removal of the PICC line. At our meeting with the doctor, he told us that I was doing fine and our next meeting would be in six weeks, when I would have a PET scan to measure the success of the treatments. The reason for waiting the six weeks was because the prior chemo and radiation treatments would continue to affect the cancer for a few more weeks; therefore, the need to wait before a PET scan.

After the 28th radiation treatment, I rang the cowbell in the patient waiting room. Ringing the cowbell was a tradition at the Mayo Clinic for all patients finishing radiation. Initially, I was not going to ring the bell because doing that would create an embarrassing moment for me. However, Kay prodded me to keep with tradition. I rang the bell with pride.

Even though I was still feeling uncomfortable due to the treatments, Kay and I were all smiles as we drove home. During the drive, we prayed for the death of all cancer cells in my body.

And my God will supply all your needs according to His riches in glory in Christ Jesus.
                              Philippians 4:19 NASB

Chapter 5

The Wait

During the ten months prior, I experienced ambivalence, curiosity, anxiety, fear, pain, discomfort, peace, and hope. Also, I cried more than I cried during the previous fifty-six years of my life. However, I was never depressed because God provided me with enough strength and patience to overcome the physical and emotional trials associated with cancer. Furthermore, my family and friends kept me as comfortable and upbeat as possible. All of that because I had cancer, which was caused by a single cell in my esophagus being stimulated by an unknown force to create an abnormal structure and to reproduce uncontrollably. An adult human body contains over 60 trillion cells; therefore, it is amazing that one cell out of trillions of cells can cause so much physical and emotional damage. Cancer is a frightening disease.

Now, I had to wait about six more weeks to see the effects of the radiation and chemo treatments on the esophageal cancer cells. Even though perseverance had never been part of my DNA, now was the time to use it.

> *And not only this, but we also exult in our tribulations, knowing that tribulation brings about perseverance; and perseverance, proven character; and proven character, hope; and hope does not disappoint, because the love of God has been poured out within our hearts through the Holy Spirit who was given to us.*
> *Romans 5:3-5 NASB*

Day 81: Well, on the second day of waiting, our smiles disappeared quickly. I noticed my left hand and arm were swollen. Pursuant to the instructions from the PICC line nurses, we immediately went to the emergency room at our local hospital. First, the local emergency doctor suspected an infection. Then, Kay phoned our Mayo doctor to tell him of my condition. The Mayo doctor and the local emergency room doctor talked on the phone and when they finished talking, I was wheeled immediately to the hospital's ultrasound unit. They were checking me for a blood clot, which was later confirmed. The blood clot was in the same vein that had the PICC line. When the Mayo nurse removed the PICC line, a small piece of clotted blood broke away from the tip of the PICC line, causing the start of a massive blood clot that eventually measured ten inches. The local doctors told us that a blood clot was a common side effect of using a PICC line. The doctors started me on an intravenously delivered blood thinner, Heparin, and admitted me into the hospital. As a fantastic caregiver and wonderful wife, Kay decided to stay with me in my hospital room.

Since the room had to be for a single occupant because my immune system was weakened by chemo, the nurses made a bed for Kay on a long built-in wooden bench. Even though she did not complain, I knew the padded bench was uncomfortable, causing her to have restless sleep. For the next few days and until my immune system recovered from the chemo, all visitors to my hospital room were required to wear face masks, including doctors, nurses, family, and friends, except of course Kay and me. Since Halloween was just a couple of weeks away, my hospital visitors got in some early witch and goblin practice by wearing masks.

Day 86: I was released from the hospital. The blood clot was still affecting the blood flow in my left arm. However, the swelling was going down. The doctors changed the blood thinner to Coumadin, which was in a capsule. I had to swallow one capsule per day. Also, I needed blood tests every few days to monitor the effects of the blood thinner. Depending on the results of the blood tests, the doctors would increase, decrease, or maintain the daily dosage of Coumadin. I prayed that the blood clot would not affect the timing for my upcoming PET scan or my cancer surgery.

Coumadin was the 12th new medicine that I had taken since being diagnosed with cancer, excluding chemo. With this drug, I had exceeded my insurance co-pay for drugs, therefore, the medicine for the remainder of the year was at no charge. I think there was a movie called "Cheaper by the Dozen." Regarding my cancer treatments, cheaper by the dozen was indeed applicable.

Day 88: Kay and I drove back to Mayo for the doctors to evaluate my blood clot. As I got out of the car, Kay told me to sit on the bench at the entrance of the Mayo Clinic while she parked the car. As she was pulling away from the curb, and unknown to her, I collapsed. The Mayo security officers and emergency medical team (EMT) quickly came to assist me. After I regained consciousness, they determined I was okay. They phoned for an ambulance to take me to the hospital for additional evaluations and then helped me into a wheelchair as we waited for the ambulance to arrive.

After parking the car, Kay tried to find me. She found me in a wheelchair surrounded by two EMTs and a security officer. Kay told them that I had fainted before and that she would mention this occurrence to the doctor. With that information, the EMTs canceled the request for an ambulance and allowed Kay to wheel me to my doctor's appointment. Kay did not let me out of the wheelchair until it was time to go home.

When we met my doctor, he confirmed that I was okay from collapsing in the clinic entryway and that the blood clot was dissolving. Additionally, we discussed that my burned esophagus and mouth sores caused throbbing pain every time I ate or drank. I told the doctor that I tried to numb the pain by drinking the medicine the nurses provided. However, the pain only subsided for a few minutes.

Since I could not eat or drink and the chemo and radiation were still affecting my body, I was dehydrated and getting weaker and weaker, which explained the reason for me fainting by the Mayo Clinic entrance. The doctor told me not to be discouraged and that the effects of chemo and radiation would last another week or so. Then, I would progressively improve. Before we left his office, the doctor scheduled another two liters of IV fluids for the afternoon and blood tests to monitor the blood thinner.

Day 100: In the morning, a good friend phoned to see if I was available for visitors at about 1:30pm. Of course I said yes, especially since Kay would be gone grocery shopping and Christine was at school. At 1:45pm, the three friends entered my house through the front door. I was sitting in my comfortable chair covered with two blankets. We had a wonderful time chatting about the good old days. There was no mention of my health situation; we simply had an enjoyable time together. At about 3:00pm, they decided to leave. As a good host, I walked them to the door. Unfortunately, I was too weak to make the round trip back to my chair. They noticed that I was having a hard time walking. Without hesitation, they grabbed my arms and led me back to my chair. At that moment, they started asking questions about my cancer. All along, they wanted to know about my health situation but were afraid to ask. I guess they did not read my CaringBridge journal entries. They stayed another half hour, talking with me and about me. I think they felt much better after knowing the details of my situation. When they departed, they made sure I stayed in my comfortable chair.

Now and for the next several weeks, I waited at home for the chemo and radiation to finish killing all the cancer cells. In addition, at my local medical clinic and under the guidance of a local specialist, I continued blood testing every few days to monitor the effects of the blood thinner. Kay and I did not drive to the Mayo Clinic or talk to a Mayo doctor for four weeks.

Chemo and radiation were now history and the side effects from the treatments were subsiding, with my weight stabilizing at 185 pounds, which was down forty pounds from my pre-cancer weight. My eating was still tenuous, but I could eat sandwiches with an extra helping of broth to wash the food down. My esophagus no longer hurt, but my stomach was still a bit squeamish, which caused some digestion discomfort. To compensate for the digestive issues, I ate at a snail's pace with very small portions. Even though some difficulties remained, I was excited that I was eating and that my physical pains were almost gone.

At that moment, I think I turned a corner. I was now thinking and praying for the hurts and needs of my family and friends, as well as for my recovery. I believed the Lord provided me with the wisdom and strength to see past my own desires and difficulties and to listen and help others in need.

I was in a better place physically and emotionally than I was a week or month prior. I continued to concentrate my time and energy on my health, but I now knew that was not enough. My daughters needed a father to help with school assignments and with understanding life, including being a playmate. Kay was in need of a husband to share household chores and to react to the good news and the not-so-good news. My grandson, Micah wanted loving hugs and a hand to hold his bottle while he ate. In addition, I had friends hurting from life's difficulties in need of a loving Christian brother. At that time, I was ready and willing to help others as much as I could.

> *Blessed be the God and Father of our Lord*
> *Jesus Christ, the Father of mercies and*
> *God of all comfort, who comforts us in*
> *all our affliction so that we will be able to*
> *comfort those who are in any affliction with*
> *the comfort with which we ourselves are*
> *comforted by God.*
> *2 Corinthians 1:3-4 NASB*

Day 108: I was eating more and more by that point, including spaghetti, beef stroganoff without the beef, brownies, eggs, tuna, and ice cream. I was walking the length of my street (half a mile) without stopping. Of course, Kay made sure I walked with someone in case of an unexpected occurrence. The night prior, I had attended a school choir concert, where my daughter, Christine, sang beautifully. It was also the first day that I got ready in the morning by myself. I was excited about my re-found independence. That was indeed a great day.

The scheduling nurse from the Mayo Clinic phoned. My surgical procedure was tentatively scheduled for December 3rd. The operation was tentative because the required pre-operation physical had to be positive. That physical included various body scans, blood tests, and heart evaluations. In addition, I had to be physically strong enough to withstand the trauma of the procedure. The testing was scheduled for the last week in November.

Day 121: It was November 27th, 2007. I had a PET scan, full body CT scan, blood tests and an electrocardiogram at the Mayo Clinic. That took about five hours. After the testing was finished, Kay and I started the one-hour and twenty-minute drove home when my cell phone rang. The ID screen on my phone identified the caller to be my radiation oncologist, which was very unusual for him to call. As a chill ran down my spine, I wondered what he wanted.

When I answered the phone, the doctor was extremely excited because he had just seen the results of my PET scan. The PET scan detected no evidence of disease (N.E.D). This was the very best outcome of chemotherapy and radiation treatments. Also, the CT scan, the blood tests, and the electrocardiogram were essentially in the normal range. The doctor still wanted to see us in the morning. However, he could not wait to tell us the fantastic news. I was cancer free, or at least the scans did not detect cancer. Kay and I were excited to tell our family and friends.

When the need warranted, our Lord provided us with an abundance of grace and mercy.

Praise the Lord, all nations;
Laud Him, all peoples!
For His lovingkindness is great toward us,
And the truth of the Lord is everlasting.
                    Psalm 117:1-2 NASB

Now, the question was whether a surgical procedure was needed. We would talk to the Mayo surgeon the next morning.

Chapter 6

Surgical Procedure

Day 124: Kay and I met with my lead Mayo doctor, a thoracic surgeon, who was very pleased with the results of the chemo and radiation treatments. As he was reviewing the results of the testing that I had just done, he often said, "Perfect, perfect, perfect!" The testing indicated that I was healthy and strong enough for the surgical operation. The scans also indicated no evidence of live cancer cells. I thought maybe the surgeon would not suggest an operation. I was wrong. He thought an operation was essential.

The surgeon started our discussion by telling us that the scans were able to detect only large masses of cancer cells and were not sensitive enough to detect a few living cancer cells. Therefore, the scans were not 100 percent effective as a diagnostic tool. As an insurance against any live cancer cells remaining, the surgeon recommended a surgical procedure to remove both the tumor and a sufficient margin of living normal cells around the affected area. That was his proposal for the best chance of keeping the disease from recurring. If the cancer returned, I would be in deep trouble because I already had a lifetime of radiation in the affected area. He offered an Ivor Lewis Esophagogastrectomy as my best option. That procedure would remove the bottom two thirds of my esophagus, the top one third of my stomach, and several surrounding lymph nodes. The remaining part of my stomach would be pulled up to attach to the remaining part of my esophagus at about collarbone level. The valve at the bottom of my stomach would be disabled, making the stomach a tube to facilitate transport of food from my mouth to my intestines; therefore, the stomach would not be able to store or help digest food. That life-saving operation would dramatically change my future eating and digestion. Also, the Mayo surgeon recommended removing my gall bladder because the CT scan identified a large gall stone. The operation would take about five hours.

I was such a lucky guy with two surgical procedures in one. I would be in the hospital for eight to ten days with a six-to-eight-week recovery period. The surgeon told us that I would probably lose another ten to twenty-five pounds before full recovery and that I would not be allowed to eat or drink for three to five days after the operation. The time was necessary for the newly formed connection between the stomach and esophagus to heal enough for liquids and solids to pass. They would keep me hydrated and nourished via an intravenous line.

As an extra insurance policy, the surgeon would insert a temporary feeding Jejunostomy tube (J-tube for short) through my abdomen wall into my small intestine. The feeding J-tube would be used in case

I started losing too much weight. Hopefully, the feeding tube would never be used. I did not think liquefied steak and potatoes fed through a plastic tube directly into my intestines would be tasty or pretty.

My procedure would be scheduled for the surgeon's first operation on Monday morning, December 3rd. The decision for the surgical procedure was Kay's and mine.

Without hesitation, we agreed to have the procedure. We wanted the cancer cells out of my body whether they were dead or alive. Also, we had an excellent secondary consultant providing surgical advice. Our brother-in-law, husband of Kay's sister, was a thoracic surgeon who had performed similar procedures. As an added note, he was also my former roommate in college. Kay and I trusted Newt, as we called him, with my life, and he recommended the procedure. Newt and Judy, Kay's sister, would travel from their home in Louisiana to the Mayo Clinic to be with us for the procedure and the subsequent hospital stay. Newt would be the liaison between Kay and the Mayo doctors and Judy would be a loving Christian sister to help in any capacity needed. Again, God provided.

With a confirmed decision for the operation, the surgeon requested immediate appointments with other specialists. We met with an endocrinologist to manage my diabetes during the operation and for a few days after the operation until I could manage the blood glucose monitoring and subsequent insulin injections on my own. We talked with a liver surgeon who would remove my gall bladder, and with an anesthesiologist who reviewed the drugs and procedures required for this type of operation. Also, I needed more blood tests to make sure my blood chemistry was in the proper ranges. Finally, I had to stop taking Coumadin because the surgeons wanted my blood to clot during and after the surgical procedure. All tests and meetings were positive. Surgery was a go in three days.

Kay and I felt strange to be thrilled about a doctor cutting into my abdomen and upper right back to restructure my digestive system; however, the other options were simply unacceptable. We were excited about that phase toward complete cure. We knew the next few weeks would be very difficult. However, we knew also that I had the best medical team, an awesome support group, the personal strength and will to cope with the operation, and most of all, a loving and merciful Lord to keep me whole.

Even though I walk through the valley of the shadow of death,
I fear no evil, for You are with me;
Your rod and Your staff, they comfort me.
Psalm 23:4 NASB

Day 126: Kay, Jennifer, Tracy, Christine, and I drove to the Mayo Clinic for hopefully a restful night before the operation. As we arrived at the Mayo Clinic at about 6:00pm, eight inches of new snow was on the ground. At 7:30pm, Newt and Judy arrived by car from Louisiana. We had a wonderful dinner, complete with enjoyable food and conversation.

At about 9:00pm, Newt phoned the Mayo surgeon. Graciously, the Mayo surgeon gave us his cell phone number for Newt to use for introducing himself and for any questions or comments prior to the operation. At the end of the phone conversation, Newt and the Mayo surgeon were in full understanding and agreement. I was a very lucky man, surrounded by my wife, children, sister-in-law, and my own private surgeon.

Day 127: December 3rd, 2007 was the day of my operation. At 6:30am, all seven of us walked across the snow-covered street from our hotel to St. Mary's Hospital, one of two hospitals used by the Mayo Clinic. The operation was scheduled for 9:00am. However, I needed to be at the hospital earlier to fill in required paperwork and to get prepped for the operation. After one last prayer and a kiss from Kay, a nurse rolled me into a surgical holding area filled with several people waiting for their time to go to various operating rooms. The only person permitted to accompany me was Newt because he was a doctor.

In the holding area, I was given a sedative to calm my nerves and we met the anesthesiologist. Thankfully, Newt was with me because he talked with the anesthesiologist about the medicines and procedures I was about to receive. I saw Newt continually shaking his head in agreement as they talked and I felt very blessed.

I do not know the time that I was finally rolled into the operating room, but Newt, who is a relative, was not allowed to join me. Inside the operating room, the nurses transferred me from my comfy gurney to a cold and hard operating table and covered me with a warm blanket to keep the chill off and to help me relax. Everyone in the room introduced themselves. However, I could not see if they were smiling or not because they wore surgical masks. Just before they put me to sleep, they confirmed who I was and the type of procedure.

The next thing I remember was seeing Kay, Jennifer, Tracy, Christine, Judy, and Newt as the nurses rolled me into my hospital room, and they were smiling. The operation went according to plan and the surgeon did not find any signs of live cancer cells. However, the definitive conclusion would come from the pathologist after the many tissue samples were evaluated.

I saw a cot in my hospital room. The cot was used by Kay and Newt as they shared time watching over me. My soul mate and my ex-roommate would stay with me 24/7. At that point, I fell asleep knowing that I was alive, safe, and in the arms of my Lord.

But as for me, I am like a green olive tree
in the house of God;
I trust in the lovingkindness of God
forever and ever.
I will give You thanks forever,
because You have done it,
And I will wait on Your name, for it is good,
in the presence of Your godly ones.
                    Psalm 52:8-9 NASB

Chapter 7

Operation Week

Day 128: Once I woke the day after the operation, I counted eight tubes coming out of my body. I did not know the purpose of each tube, but I did not care. Also, I had a seven-inch vertical incision on my abdomen and a six-inch horizontal curved incision on my upper right back about arm pit level. Both visible incisions were glued shut instead of using sutures or staples. However, I was told that the doctors used sutures to close internal incisions and connections.

At about 9:00am, the nurses came into my hospital room to get me up into a nearby chair. The nurses were wonderful as they took excellent care of me, but, at that moment, they were a bit aggressive in getting me mobile before I was ready. I thought they could have let me rest for at least a day after such a traumatic operation. As the nurses helped me to the chair, all eight tubes and the intravenous stand containing several bags of medicines came with me. I felt like an alien connected to a life support system in a sci-fi movie.

As soon as they sat me in the chair, I experienced an intense pain in my abdomen. The nurses quickly paged "the pain doctor." The doctor came into my room accompanied by a flock of interns. After a few questions, the doctor apologized for my discomfort, explained that the Mayo philosophy was to prevent pain because it inhibited recovery from operations, and then, increased the dosage of pain medicine through an IV tube. In a few seconds, the pain was gone.

I thought sitting in a chair would be enough for the first day. However, the nurses came into my room again later with the plan of getting me to walk the halls. That day, I walked four different times for about fifty yards per walk. I walked with my buddies: Newt, Kay, and the portable IV stand.

Day 131: All tubes were removed except one IV line. I was taken to an X-ray lab to evaluate the newly formed stomach-esophagus connection. The technicians took several X-rays as I drank a chalky textured barium contrast and ate a barium cookie. The X-ray pictures showed no leaks at the connection. After three-and-a-half days of no liquid or food entering my mouth, I was allowed to eat, starting with a clear liquid diet followed the next day by a full liquid diet.

Pursuant to the instructions from my nurses, Newt and my IV stand walked with me in the halls around the perimeter of the fifth floor of the hospital. We walked three different times for a total distance of about a half mile. We were told that four other patients on that floor had the same operation as I had. Unfortunately, we did not meet them due to hospital privacy rules.

I was having trouble sleeping, so the nurses gave me some medicine to help me sleep. After I took the sleeping pills, they had trouble waking me the next morning. Kay suggested reducing the sleep medicine dosage in half, which the nurses did.

Day 133: Newt and Judy left for their home in Louisiana. They were an awesome support to us and we could not thank them enough. Now, I had to manage my recovery without my private surgeon.

My Mayo surgeon shared with us the results of the pathology report. The pathologist found living cancer cells in one of the twenty-three lymph nodes that the surgeons removed, which confirmed the need for the operation. However, there was no evidence of cancer in the tumor or margins removed from my stomach and esophagus. The surgeon was very pleased with these results as well as with my post-operation progress. In fact, he said that I probably could be discharged in two days. My body was now N.E.D (no evidence of disease). God had abundantly supplied us with all of our needs and we did not take it for granted. Our faith had been our foundation for the past four-and-a-half months, and we surely would have crumbled without Him.

And we know that God causes all things to work together for good to those who love God, to those who are called according to His purpose.
                              Romans 8:28 NASB

Day 135: On Tuesday, December 11, 2007, eight days after the operation, Kay and I left St. Mary's Hospital for home at 11:45am. Before we left the hospital, the nurses warned us of the dreaded "Dumping Syndrome," which is diarrhea. Since the food I ate went directly into my small intestines without being stored or partially digested in my stomach, my new digestive system would "dump" any overload of carbohydrates or dairy products. Therefore, I had to eat small portions of food several times a day. Essentially, I would be grazing instead of eating festive meals.

The Mayo Clinic staff was awesome with their understanding, skills, and performance, and they had a gracious and caring attitude toward my family and me. As we left the hospital, they sent us home with a list of emergency phone numbers, a list of instructions, a bottle of pain pills, a bottle of sleeping pills, and an appointment to see the surgeon in one week.

Chapter 8

Living With A *Stomaphagus*

Day 134: Praise the Lord! I was home sleeping in my own bed. It was only eight days since the surgical procedure and I was very weak. As an example of how weak I was, I had to use a chair in the shower to sit as I washed for the day because I could not stand without support for more than a couple of minutes. For the next several weeks, I had to dedicate myself to rest and regaining some of my previous strength and stamina.

On blog sites for esophageal cancer, Tracy discovered a new word referring to my abnormal digestive track. Since esophageal cancer survivors do not have a normal stomach or esophagus, the reconstructed food pathway was called a *stomaphagus*. This new word did not resolve any of my physical or emotional issues, but the name did bring some fun and humor into our lives.

Kay and I started a conversation about how, what, and when I could eat. I needed to get more liquid, calories, protein, and other nutrients into my system, but how with a stomaphagus? My medical team told me to eat in small quantities several times a day. That was excellent advice, except they did not say how small or at what times or what types of food. Kay and I reasoned that trial and error would be our plan for determining the best eating method for my stomaphagus. That was not a very good plan, but we knew of no other choices.

Day 138: Kay and I attended an end of the year luncheon at my work. I was still too weak to walk by myself, so Kay had to hold my arm as we entered the luncheon area. We were greeted with a spontaneous round of applause and, during the clapping, joy filled my heart. That was the first time I had seen many of my work colleagues in over four months. Kay and I appreciated the time with my work friends. After about an hour, we left for home because I was getting very tired. I missed working and socializing with my colleagues. Hopefully, I would be able to return to work soon, but not in 2007.

Day 140: Last August when the final diagnosis was confirmed, the doctors educated us about all the necessary treatments. However, nobody mentioned 24/7 hiccups, fainting, blood clots, dehydration, loss of driving privileges, dumping, etc. These are some of the unpredictable adventures that come with esophageal cancer. I experienced all of them, including some others that I could not remember. Yes, loss of memory was another one.

Last night, another unexpected event occurred. At about 10:30pm, I was feeling hypoglycemic, which is a condition associated with low blood sugar. As all diabetics understand, a few swallows of orange juice usually bring the blood sugars back to normal. However, I had a stomaphagus. Instead of feeling normal, I started to sweat and shake uncontrollably. Unfortunately, Kay was two houses down the street, enjoying a pre-Christmas night out with some friends and Christine was at a movie with her friends. I was home alone and not thinking clearly. I started to panic. Luckily, I was able to pick up my cell phone to speed dial Kay. I was only able to say, "Help." She ran home to find me on the sofa and non-coherent.

After a couple of minutes to assess my medical condition, Kay pricked my finger and used a glucometer to determine my blood sugar level. The screen on the glucometer displayed a blood sugar level of 25 mg/dl, which was dangerously low. She tried to feed me sugar without success. We did not have an emergency syringe filled with glucagon which, when injected, would increase my blood sugar level. Lacking any other good options available to her, Kay dialed 911 on the house phone and the Mayo emergency number on her cell phone. Neither of us had ever experienced this type of reaction.

The paramedics and police arrived at about 10:50pm. Kay explained the situation to the paramedics about my cancer, recent operation, and very low blood sugar. The paramedics pricked my finger again to test my blood sugar level. Indeed, a dangerously low blood sugar level was confirmed. Then, the paramedics talked to the Mayo doctor on Kay's cell phone. The doctor and paramedics quickly agreed to a plan. The paramedics injected a glucagon solution into my arm, connected a saline IV line, and had me breathe oxygen rich gas. Then, they transported me to the emergency room at a local hospital.

By the time we arrived at the hospital, my blood sugar level was just about normal and I was relaxed. The most plausible cause for this scary event was low blood sugar, dehydration, and sipping orange juice, which was cold and acidic. I guess that my stomaphagus was not yet able to accept orange juice.

After a few hours of monitoring my blood sugar level and watching my reactions, the emergency room doctor discharged me from the hospital at 4:00am. However, we had another problem. Since Kay rode in the ambulance with me, we did not have a car to take us home. Also, since I left home without socks and shoes, I could not walk outside, especially since the temperature was below freezing. Again, the nurses came to our rescue. They gave me two pairs of hospital disposable slippers to wear and they called a taxi for us. These were simple solutions to awkward problems.

On a side note, Christine arrived home about one minute before the ambulance and two police cars stopped at our house. When she saw the police cars and ambulance, she started to scream and cry. She thought the worst. Thankfully, her friends and their mom, a nurse, were able to comfort her until the paramedics stabilized me. Once she saw Kay and me, she started to relax. She went to her friend's house for the remainder of the night and they played

Monopoly to relieve the stress. I was so happy to give her a comforting hug when I saw her the next morning.

Day 149: It was Christmas day. Kay and I celebrated the birth of Jesus Christ with our three daughters, two sons-in-law, and our precious grandson. That was a special day of thanksgiving, prayer, and joy.

> *But the angel said to them, "Do not be*
> *afraid; for behold, I bring you good news*
> *of great joy which will be for all the people;*
> *for today in the city of David there has been*
> *born for you a Savior, who is Christ the*
> *Lord. This will be a sign for you: you will*
> *find a baby wrapped in cloths and lying in*
> *a manager." And suddenly there appeared*
> *with the angel a multitude of the heavenly*
> *host praising God and saying,*
> *"Glory to God in the highest, And on*
> *earth peace among men with whom He*
> *is pleased."*
> *Luke 2:10-14 NASB*

Day 150: The day after Christmas was a very different type of day. I caught the stomach flu, or should it be called "the stomaphagus flu?" Yes, the flu! I was vomiting, causing even more weight loss and dehydration. I was already down sixty pounds to 165 pounds, and the doctors wanted me at 180 pounds. Because of my weight loss issue and the possibility of getting too dehydrated, Kay phoned the Mayo emergency number. The doctor instructed us to use the feeding J-tube port to inject water into my body to prevent excessive dehydration and then, to make an appointment with our Mayo surgeon as soon as I recovered from the flu.

Day 158: It was January 2nd, 2008. My recovery from the surgical procedure had been more difficult than I expected. Getting the "stomaphagus flu" did not help. My plan was to return to work at least for half days during the first week in January. Well, the timing for that plan was unrealistic because I was still at home. Now, my amended plan was to return to work part-time the first week in February.

I was now down to 155 pounds. We needed to do something different very quickly since our trial and error eating plan was not working. Pursuant to my doctor's instruction, I started using the feeding J-tube to supplement my eating. The doctors were concerned that I was not getting enough fluids, nutrition, and calories. We calculated that I was ingesting only about 800 calories and drinking only about two glasses of fluid per day. I needed to eat a minimum of 2,100 calories and drink at least five glasses of fluid. We had to reverse the weight loss and dehydration trend. We started to slowly pump, into the J-tube, 1.26 liters per day of a doctor pre-scribed fluid containing 1,500 calories and various nutrients. Every day, I was using the feeding J-tube for seventeen hours from 4:00pm to 9:00am. That allowed me to eat my current 800 calories and drink two glasses of water via my mouth so that my stomaphagus could continue to regain functionality. The combination of the feeding J-tube and oral eating provided the needed nourishment for me to start gaining some weight.

Since I was using the feeding J-tube, I needed to have a home nurse and a local dietician. My local general internist helped us find them. First, they instructed Kay and me on how to use the feeding J-tube, the IV pump, the bottle of prescribed fluid, and the logbook recording my daily food and fluid intake. Once we learned the essentials, we were on our own to facilitate my daily nourishment. The home nurse met with us for about one hour every few days. She checked my vital signs and changed the bandages holding the feeding J-tube connection in place. The dietician periodically reviewed the intake logbook and talked to our home nurse to adjust the feeding J-tube prescribed fluid, as required. During her scheduled visits, the home nurse also answered any questions that Kay or I had concerning my medical condition.

At that time, I was both frustrated and encouraged. I was frustrated due to the difficulty in recovering from the operation and from my eating issues. Certainly, the radiation and chemo treatments had

had a negative impact on my recovery, but still, I thought that I could have been feeling stronger by this point. In my short fifty-six-year lifetime, I had had several surgical procedures and recovered from each of those procedures with relative ease. That last procedure humbled me. The Mayo surgeon said that the recovery from that procedure was one of the six most difficult. He was spot-on.

At the same time as being frustrated, I was encouraged and optimistic by the positive prognosis of N.E.D and by my return to normal life being within sight. If the surgeon was correct with respect to the average time for recovery being eight weeks, I had another four weeks before normalcy returned and four more weeks was not a long time. As a matter of fact, six months from diagnosis to complete recovery was not a major burden. I felt very blessed to be in this situation.

Day 162: I was feeling much better and gained five pounds in the previous four days. By using the feeding J-tube, I had started a positive recovery cycle. Again, I was blessed with the wonders of medical science and the powerful healing touch of my Lord.

> *Then they cried out to the Lord in*
> *their trouble;*
> *He saved them out of their distresses.*
> *He sent His word and healed them,*
> *And delivered them from their destructions.*
> *Psalm 107:19-20 NASB*

Day 173: Kay and I went to the Mayo Clinic for testing and doctors' appointments. The test results and the meetings were very positive. The cancer was still in remission and my stomaphagus appeared to be okay. The doctors said that my blood clot was considered an incidental event, therefore, I did not need to continue taking a blood thinner. Even though my recovery was slow as related to my timetable, the doctors said that I was on par with others who had experienced the same treatments. That suggested that I was average. It was good to be average.

Day 187: It was February 1, 2008 and I went to work for four hours. I attended a one-hour meeting and then met with colleagues for various updates. I enjoyed being with friends. However, the day was more tiring than anticipated. From that half-day experience, I learned to be very careful about not overdoing it. I asked some work friends and Kay to continue to watch me through the next few weeks. If they saw any signs of fatigue, they should shut me down for a time of rest. I promised to obey them unconditionally. Kay picked me up from work at 11:30am for the ten-minute drive home and then I had a two-hour nap.

I continued to use the feeding J-tube about fifteen hours every day. The current plan was to work half days until I was weaned off of the feeding J-tube. I still was not allowed to drive, therefore, Kay drove me back and forth to work.

Day 208: Kay and I drove to Mayo for a CT scan and scheduled meetings with the surgeon and medical oncologist. The good news was that the cancer was still in remission and that I did not need another chemotherapy treatment. The medical oncologist said that since there was no evidence of live cancer cells, chemotherapy probably would do more harm to my body than good. In addition, we told the surgeon of my continued problem with swallowing solid foods. He thought that scar tissue was possibly growing at the stomach-esophagus connection narrowing the channel, which was a common concern for many other similar patients. The best way to check was with an endoscopy. For the fifth time, I would have to swallow a camera attached to a tube. The doctor scheduled the endoscopy for Monday, February 25.

Day 211: The endoscopy surgeon did not see any narrowing or scar tissue in my stomaphagus, but decided anyway to do a dilatation. A dilatation was a procedure of inflating a balloon in the passageway to stretch the tissue, allowing for a bigger hole. Since I was sedated, the procedure for me was more of an inconvenience than a problem. The dilatation seemed to work because that night I was able to eat more solid food.

Day 247: It was April Fool's day. For me, it was not a day for practical jokes, but a milestone day. For the first time in over eight months, I drove myself to a full day of work. I was slowly but continuously improving. By this point, four months had passed since my operation and I was able to eat a larger variety of foods, though always at a very low volume (one half to one cup per sitting). I was walking a half mile per day without resting and was helping Kay with minor chores around the house.

There were still some issues though in my daily life. For example, I still hooked up to a feeding J-tube to supplement my food intake, had occasional coughing spasms, had daily intestinal cramps after eating too fast or too much or not the correct food, and took Tylenol for aches and pains, Ambien for sleep, and Pepcid for stomaphagus acids. The doctors were correct as I needed much more time for full recovery. Hopefully, by the end of summer, I would be fully recovered.

After reading the above, it may sound that I was depressed. On the contrary, I was happy and blessed. My gracious and merciful Lord had embraced me with cancer remission and with inner peace and I was still blessed with a marvelous support group and medical team. During my trials with cancer, I learned so much from my Lord and my supporters. That excited me to live the rest of my life as a better person with focus on "self-giving" instead of "self-seeking." I prayed every day to find and walk the correct path toward God's truth.

> *O send out Your light and Your truth,*
> *let them lead me;*
> *Let them bring me to Your holy hill*
> *And to Your dwelling places.*
> *Psalm 43:3 NASB*

Day 299: At 5:00am, Kay and I drove to the Mayo Clinic for tests and doctors' meetings. My first appointment was at 7:00am, therefore, an early wake-up was required. I had a CT scan, a chest X-ray, a meeting with the medical oncologist, and a meeting with my surgeon. The day ended with an ice cream cone on the drive home at 3:00pm.

The CT scan and the chest X-ray were both clean, showing no evidence of cancer. My medical oncologist said my recovery was excellent and she wanted me to push myself harder regarding more eating, drinking, and exercise. She said the normal complete recovery was between nine to twelve months. I was about six months into recovery and weighed 165 pounds, which was ten pounds above my lowest weight. My stomaphagus was almost fully healed, therefore, it was time to regain my strength and stamina. She said my appetite should return with more activity. I wished Kay did not hear the doctor's comments because it got Kay on a campaign to get me to sweat.

The meeting with the surgeon was somewhat more exciting. He removed the feeding J-tube from my abdomen. That meant no more feeding J-tube and no more home nurse. My surgeon reiterated the comments made by the medical oncologist when he said that I must push myself to exercise and become more active. Again, Kay heard those comments. Now my problem was: how could I reel in a wife who was on a sweat crusade for me?

The report from the Mayo Clinic was wonderful. The doctor put me on a three-month monitoring regimen, which meant that my next trip to Mayo would be at the end of August. Hopefully, the cancer would remain in remission.

Chapter 9

Cured

My Mayo Clinic medical oncologist suggested a five-year post-operation monitoring schedule to evaluate for recurrence of the esophageal cancer. For the first two years after the surgical procedure, I would be evaluated every three months, and for the next two years after that, I would be evaluated every six months. The final evaluation would be on the fifth year anniversary after the operation. The plan was to use either a chest X-ray or a CT scan at each evaluation, but not both. The reasons to use X-rays and CT scans was because a CT scan displays more details of the body than an

X-ray. However, a CT scan requires 100 times more radiation than X-rays. Also, CT scans occasionally showed a false positive, requiring unnecessary extra testing. My medical oncologist preferred to use X-rays as much as possible. However, she also recognized the value of the details revealed in a CT scan. If the fifth year evaluation showed no evidence of cancer, then there was a very minimal chance the esophageal cancer would return. I would be cured.

Day 384: My third post-operation quarterly exam at the Mayo Clinic was excellent. The cancer was still in remission. However, the doctor told me that she would like to see a few more pounds on my bones. I was at 165 pounds and holding. Therefore, the doctor wanted to do some additional testing to better understand my issues with swallowing, digestion, and lack of weight gain.

All tests of my stomaphagus, kidneys, and bladder supported a healthy, fully functional male. The doctor concluded that I simply needed to continue on the present plan of grazing, exercise, and enjoying life. Maybe 165 pounds was the new normal for me.

Day 407: Life was not perfect. I had to endure another setback after being diagnosed with Shingles. Shingles is a viral infection of the nerve roots. Due to having chickenpox as a youngster, the chickenpox virus remained in my body, staying dormant in the nerve roots. When the immune system is weakened, coupled with stress or a long-term disease, the chickenpox virus becomes active. Chickenpox does not recur, but instead, the virus awakens as Shingles. Shingles is a localized rash, following a major nerve on only one side of the body. It is marked by fluid-filled blisters, which last for a few weeks. My blisters followed the right side femoral nerve starting at my lower back and ending at my knee. The doctor put me on an antiviral medicine, Acyclovir. I swallowed one pill five times a day and was able to continue working, even under the aggravation of itching and minor pain.

Day 503: Praise the Lord! My fourth post-operation quarterly checkup at the Mayo Clinic went well and my test results were excellent. I was one year N.E.D. Also, a few days prior, I had my yearly health examination at 3M Company's medical clinic. Again, all test results were excellent. The doctors said I was perfect. Kay thought the doctors meant the test results were perfect. However, I still think the doctors meant I was perfect.

Because of my stomaphagus, the recovery from cancer was challenging. I still did not have an appetite and I continued to graze, with frequent abdominal discomfort. I wanted to eat and exercise more, but I had very limited success. Christine said I was a buff 165 pounds. Maybe buff was too kind. However, I did have more energy, was standing straighter with more confidence, and was lifting light weights. Maybe buff was accurate!

Day 621: My fifth post-operation quarterly checkup at the Mayo Clinic was excellent. I was still N.E.D and my spirits remained high.

To better enjoy eating, the doctor suggested I take Prevacid, an acid blocker. The doctor said the medicine should help with reflux. It definitely helped reduce burping and coughing during and after meals. However, it did not completely eliminate the issues.

On a very positive note, I started playing golf again. It was April 2009. Almost two years had passed since the last time I played golf. I lost seventy-five yards on my drives and my handicap increased a few strokes. Even though my game was not as good as pre-cancer, I enjoyed being outside and playing golf with friends on a beautiful piece of real estate. Life was good!

Day 1,870: It had been almost five years since the surgical procedure. All quarterly and semi-annual evaluations at the Mayo Clinic had been excellent. Every CT scan and X-ray showed no evidence of disease. All meetings with the Mayo doctors were positive and uneventful, therefore, I fast forward to my last evaluation at the Mayo Clinic.

My CT scan was clean, which meant I was still N.E.D. My weight was now at 170 pounds. During this final meeting with my medical oncologist, I asked if I was cured. She was very hesitant to use the term, but after much persuasion, I got her to say, "You are cured."

She discharged me from the Mayo Clinic Medical Oncology Service. I will miss seeing and talking with my medical team at the Mayo Clinic. They were very friendly and helpful to Kay and me. However, I will not miss the drive to Mayo.

Halleluiah! Finally, I was cured. My formula for cure was relatively simple, or at least, I thought so. I used four distinct components as follows:

• FAITH: The first meaningful thing that Kay and I did after I was diagnosed with esophageal cancer was to pray. I needed the Lord to grant me peace, strength, patience, grace, and mercy to endure the physical and emotional challenges relevant to my cancer treatments and care. I needed the

Lord to grant me His healing touch. My Lord was and still is the Great Physician. The first key to a cure was to turn unconditionally total control of my life over to my Lord, Jesus Christ.

Thus says the Lord,
"Cursed is the man who trusts
in mankind
And makes flesh his strength,
And whose heart turns away
from the Lord.
For he will be like a bush in the desert
And will not see when prosperity comes,
But will live in stony wastes in the
wilderness,
A land of salt without inhabitant.
Jeremiah 17:5, 6 NASB

• FAMILY: I needed to find a close relative willing to be my caregiver and advocate. During the cancer treatments and recovery, my emotions and physical state were overwhelming, which prohibited me from listening and thinking clearly and objectively. If I did not have an advocate, I very likely would have made poor decisions.

Therefore, I needed someone to watch over me. In my situation, Kay was obviously my special angel. In addition, my daughters (the fabulous three), brothers, and in-laws interrupted their busy lives to help Kay and me. They pledged their time and energy to assist us, even traveling great distances. The second key to a cure was to embrace an advocate and other family members willing and able to provide 24/7 help.

* FRIENDS: I wanted to be surrounded by faithful friends because I could not have managed my emotional and spiritual state in isolation. I tried to keep an open and frequent communication channel with them by maintaining an up-to-date journal on the CaringBridge web site. In return, our friends sent thousands of messages, visited our home, helped with domestic chores, and filled our freezer with excellent dinners. All of the messages and visits helped to raise my spirit and to overcome the many physical and emotional

trials. Our friends were a blessing for Kay and me. They were the third key to a cure.

• PHYSICIANS: A cancer patient must find a medical team experienced and gifted to provide the best-of-the-best medical science and care. There are many renowned cancer facilities around the world. In my situation, the Mayo Clinic was definitely the correct choice. During the course of my cancer treatments and eventual cure, I met with more than 100 medical specialists. Considering the need to have timely access to those doctors and medical tests, the medical facility must also have a well-defined system to schedule appointments within hours, not weeks. The Mayo Clinic with a staff of 25,000 exemplifies all of the above and is one of the best medical facilities in the United States. The fourth key to a cancer cure is to find a state-of-the-art cancer clinic that will correctly treat and remove the cancer as quickly, professionally, and compassionately as possible.

Chapter 10

An Advocate's Perspective
(Written by Kay)

As we talked at the coffee shop the morning of Mike's diagnosis, I realized that he would need someone to care for him not only physically, but also emotionally and spiritually. I was thankful that God had given me a husband who was optimistic in his general outlook on life, and who was always determined to accomplish a task after setting his mind to it. This would serve him well in the coming months. As we prayed that morning, we knew our prayer was heard by the Living God, Who knows our afflictions and gives us what we need to endure them.

As I look back on the years before Mike's cancer diagnosis, I see that God was preparing me in advance for the job that would be required of me during and after Mike's cancer ordeal. Between 1992 and 2003, Mike had double knee replacements and one knee revision after the initial replacement wore out. All of that took place at the Mayo Clinic, which gave us knowledge of how Mayo operated and also confidence in the abilities of the physicians. In 1999 and 2004, my mom had hip replacement operations at the Mayo Clinic as well, and came to our home for "Nurse Kay" to care for her until she recovered. Therefore, I had acquired first-hand knowledge of how to take care of someone after a serious surgical procedure and during their stay in the hospital. So in 2007 when Mike was diagnosed with a very serious cancer, we decided to use the Mayo Clinic where, previously, we had positive results and I felt comfortable with the surroundings. In addition, Mike was already established as a patient at Mayo and I did not have to take precious time away from getting the treatments started by researching different cancer centers.

Being Mike's advocate was one of the most important parts of my caring for him. Whether it was asking questions of doctors and sometimes not settling for their answers, making sure Mike had everything he needed during his hospital stay, screening calls and visits, or occasionally making demands of doctors and nurses that was out of character for me, I felt all of these things were imperative for Mike to be comfortable and cared for properly. As Mike alluded to previously, his radiation oncologist, whom we saw often, probably hated to see me coming. Most days I would get out my long list of questions and the doctor would patiently go through it with me. In one instance when my friend had suggested Baclofen for hiccups, I asked the doctor if we could try it. He said that he had never heard of that medicine and that it was not one they ever used for radiation or chemo side effects. However, he immediately went to his computer and looked it up. He said, "It won't hurt Mr. Lynn, so let's try it." As a side note, it took Mike's hiccups away and he felt 100 percent better. Another example was during one of Mike's fluid infusions. I looked at the fluid they were giving him and it was a glucose/saline solution, not a good idea for a diabetic. The nurse had mistakenly given him the wrong solution. Constant vigilance and perseverance (nagging) was essential so that Mike could concentrate solely on his health and trust that I was doing the rest of what needed to be done.

> *Consider it all joy, my brethren, when you encounter various trials, knowing that the testing of your faith produces endurance (perseverance). And let endurance have its perfect result, so that you may be perfect and complete, lacking in nothing.*
> *James 1:2-4 NASB*

Caring for someone who is not always able to communicate what they need can be frustrating and stressful. Mike would often have times when I could see something was wrong, but he would not talk. I would first take his blood sugar to rule out a high or low level, and then I would guess and pray at the same time as to what I should do next. I would later ask him if he could hear me and why would he not answer? He would say that he could hear me, but that he was focusing on getting through the episode. That ability to focus and tune out everything around him was a good thing for him, but a scary thing for me and the rest of the family. I suspect that many of you alpha males can identify with this character trait. Mike's moods were, of course, up and down from day to day and sometimes hour to hour. It was important for Christine and me to be kind and understanding when he seemed grouchy and impatient.

Jennifer, Tracy, and Christine were an enormous help to Mike and me. Whenever they were visiting, Mike would perk up, and I could see that it was emotionally helping him to cope. The love and support they gave was invaluable to us. Jennifer surprised us with visits (she lived four hours from us), Tracy had a colicky two-month-old, and Christine was only fourteen years old. They put aside their own problems to be always upbeat, positive, and available. They were and continue to be a source of great joy in our lives.

During the first nine weeks after Mike's diagnosis, Mike and I were at Mayo almost every day, not including weekends. I worried about who was going to care for Christine and keep up with all of her activities, and I thought about all the things I needed to be doing to keep the household running properly. I made lists of grocery items and other things I needed to purchase for that week, yet I knew I would never be able to get it all done. Thankfully, I did not need to worry for very long! I started to get calls from many dear friends offering to cook, clean, shop, garden, snowplow, take Mike for a drive, take me out for lunch, visit, and so many other offers of support, both physical and emotional. This outpouring of love was so overwhelming and therapeutic.

Although I was initially reluctant to receive their help, thinking it would be a burden for them, I soon realized that we would not be able to get through the next few months without them. Truth be told, I did not think I could have stopped them! This was also a way for them to be a part of our journey and know that we loved them and valued their friendship. Together, Mike and I would read the cards of love and encouragement that were sent to him from all over the world, and in fact, we still have them all. It is impossible to convey how necessary our support system was in beating the cancer and shining the light of Christ during some very dark days.

Be devoted to one another in brotherly love;
give preference to one another in honor
Romans 12:10 NASB

Arguably, the hardest part of being a caregiver is watching the one you love suffer day after day. I found no way to avoid it, so I prayed continuously for Mike's relief from pain and discomfort and had many other cries of supplication and praise. In our case, we did not know if Mike would survive, and the uncertainty of that prognosis was difficult. However, the peace of mind that God gave us allowed us to go through the many months of treatment and recovery without fear. I knew that whatever happened, life or death, God was sovereign and that I could trust Him completely. This confidence allowed me to sleep at night and to navigate each day with the constant vigilance and energy I needed. I am convinced that a positive attitude, determination, and a sense of inner peace that only God can give for both the patient and caregiver, are essential to surviving esophageal cancer.

Chapter 11

Social Support Studies

There are many published scientific studies validating that my formula for cancer survival was not a one-of-a-kind success. The studies present a significant positive contribution from faith, family, and friends on cancer survival rates, including esophageal cancer.

One study[1] analyzed the survival results of more than 1 million cancer patients from 2004 through 2008. The results disclosed that married patients were 20 percent more likely to survive from cancer than unmarried patients. Thank you, Kay!

Another study[2] concluded that identifying and treating depression in cancer patients improved the probability for survival by over 19 percent. After reviewing this study, I gave praise to my family, friends, and Lord for providing me the strength, encouragement, and love required to maintain a balanced emotional state. They helped keep me from anxiety and depression issues.

The Lord is my strength and my shield;
My heart trusts in Him, and I am helped;
Therefore my heart exults,
And with my song I shall thank Him.
                                        Psalm 28:7 NASB

I mention these two studies, not because they are the "holy grail" of psychological oncology, but because I just happened to read them and they reinforced the need for social support in the overall treatment of cancer. Also, the two studies helped me understand the reason I needed continuous communication with my support team.

I am neither a psychologist nor a well-read expert in this field. However, I did experience the benefits of a caring group during my path to cure. The two mentioned studies indicate a strong adverse connection between socially isolated and depressed cancer patients and survival. I have read about the human species being tribal people in need of relationships, especially during times of distress. Cancer patients are definitely in need of help, not only from medical professionals, but also from a caring community.

Cancer patients require a support group to help with critical care issues such as: clear communication with medical professionals, adherence to timely treatments, maintenance of nutrition intake, and simply rides to appointments. They are not only vulnerable to physical suffering but also to emotional and spiritual distress. I hope and pray for cancer centers and medical professionals to be more intentional in analyzing the patient's social structure. If the doctors sense a social disconnect, maybe some guidance or even expert psychological help would improve the ability to survive. Indeed, my cancer outcome benefited from my social support because they helped improve my spirit and offered me hope.

Chapter 12

Post Cancer

During my recovery from the surgical procedure, I had the opportunity to reflect on how I was living and more importantly, to pray about how I ought to live. In my pre-cancer life, I had faith in a sovereign, triune God and in salvation. I thought that I was a good Christian by praying daily, attending church on Sunday, reading the Bible, tithing my money and time, and befriending many other honest and moral people. Also, I understood that I was a decent person, obeying laws and creating a good life for my family. However, I was prideful and self-confident and, in most situations, I used self-control to rule my life. I believed I was saved by Christian actions and good works, but I was not living by faith in Jesus Christ and did not have a contrite heart.

On the day I was diagnosed with cancer, my responses to life's challenges changed. I was broken and brought to my knees. At that point, I repented from my sins and finally recognized the need to turn my life totally over to my Lord, Jesus Christ. Then I asked myself, "How can I better live in faith?" I turned to the Scriptures for guidance.

Oh give thanks to the Lord,
call upon His name;
Make known His deeds among the peoples.
Sing to Him, sing praises to Him;
Speak of all His wonders.
Psalm 105:1,2 NASB

What could I do? How could I make known what God had done? I believed my cancer experience was a learning opportunity for me. Yes, my cure from cancer was a physical and medical success, but it was also a gift from God for me to praise Him and to witness for Him. God gave me more time on earth to share myself, my cancer experiences, and my spiritual growth with others. I needed to find an appropriate mechanism to share my story and the hope that we have in Christ.

I assumed that many, if not most cancer patients struggle with post-cancer priorities. I believed that resetting, or at least rethinking, priorities was a natural side effect of cancer. As people live their lives, self-imposed priorities are set and occasionally modified with time. Many different actions and reactions create the need for priority modifications such as a change in work, family make-up, age, address, health, etc. I am not different from most people. I have had dozens, if not more, priority changes during my life. Being diagnosed and subsequently cured of cancer caused me to reconsider my priorities.

I talked with Kay about my thoughts. I told her that I had been so very blessed throughout my life with a fabulous family, wonderful friends, a beautiful place to live, an excellent work experience, and a loving, gracious, and merciful God. At this time in my life, I wanted to find a way to give back more to the community. It was time to reset my priorities. I wanted to help other cancer patients manage the physical, emotional, and spiritual issues encountered with cancer. In addition, I wanted to help underprivileged people in our community. Kay agreed with my thinking and offered her help.

After being in agreement with Kay, the first thing I did to reset my priorities was to retire from 3M Company where I worked for over thirty-two years. Even though I truly enjoyed my colleagues and work assignments, I needed more time for my new mission. May 29th, 2009 was my last day at work. It was a sad day for me.

The next thing Kay and I did was to spend more time at a local ministry focused on nourishing the physical and spiritual needs of the underprivileged. My son-in-law, Pastor Chris was the key person in getting Kay and me involved. Not only did Kay and I volunteer at this ministry, but also we gained the support of our home church in providing other volunteers and in sponsoring programs at this ministry.

Next, I contacted a few cancer organizations to gain insight into their needs and how I could help cancer patients, especially esophageal cancer patients. The cancer groups mentioned several opportunities to help such as: financial support, mentoring programs, political activism, providing transportation to and from appointments, fund raising, and joining their board of directors. I chose to help by donating money to several cancer organizations and by volunteering at four different cancer organizations with broad reach throughout the United States. At this point, I spend time transporting patients to and from their medical appointments, as well as mentoring esophageal cancer patients and their caregivers. If the patient lives near my home, I communicate with them face-to-face, if possible. If the patient lives far from my home, I communicate via phone and e-mail.

Another priority reset was spending more time socializing and golfing with my friends. Even more important, I spend time with them when they are in trouble or hurting. On several occasions, I was privileged to be with friends as they grieved for the passing of loved ones or as they recovered from surgical procedures and illnesses.

One of my most important priority resets was and still is being a grandfather. Kay and I have four grandchildren. We devote as much time as possible to being open, gracious, and available grandparents. Spending time with grandkids is awesome.

I am glad that I retired early to enjoy the times being a husband, father, grandfather, friend, and volunteer. Being cured of esophageal cancer provided me with the understanding and opportunity to change my priorities in a very positive and Christian way. Life in general and God's plan for me were and still are amazing.

Real and everlasting hope is only provided from God, therefore, as I end my cancer story, I have one more scripture verse to share.

Now may the God of hope fill you with
all joy and peace in believing, so that you
will abound in hope by the power of the
Holy Spirit.

Romans 15:13NASB

Endnotes

1. Aizer et al, "Marital status and survival in patients with cancer." Journal of Clinical Oncology 31:3869-3876. 2013
2. Gallo et al, "The effect of primary care practice-based depression intervention on mortality in older adults: A randomized trial." Annals of Internal Medicine 146:689-698. 2007

CPSIA information can be obtained at www.ICGtesting.com
Printed in the USA
BVOW05s0937030414

349564BV00001B/2/P